AF326658

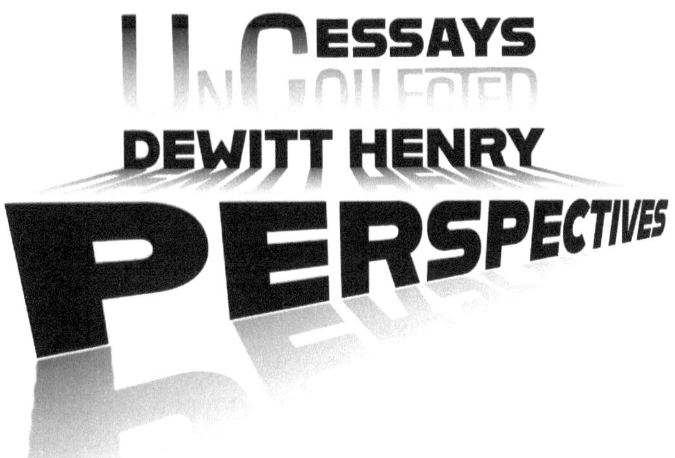

What If ?
Thoughts on Tille Olsen
First Love   Sever Hall   On Fact and Fiction
Face to Face   Memories of Henry Bromell
Remembering James Alan McPherson   The Saga of a Chair
Promises to Keep

Uncollected ESSAYS

DEWITT HENRY

PERSPECTIVES

"*First Love* is some of the best writing about sex I've ever read."

—**Cassandra Atherton,** author of
A Perfect Life

"This essayistic memoir is all about lived life, of perspectives on the present, on the past. Of place, purpose, and experience. Of professional life, of university teaching. Of the writing life. Of the prestigious literary magazine—*Ploughshares*. On its start-up. Of the nature of literature. Of writer friends. Of famous writer friends. On the reality of being human. On aging. On religious and philosophical perspectives. On young love and lust. On marriage. On lived life, existence, with its many complications and expressions. This hybrid of memoir and essay is a tour de force in breadth as well as depth."

—**Jack Smith,** author of *Amor Fati*

"*Perspectives* is as multifaceted as a diamond's surface—Henry reflects on a wide range of topics and events, on family and youth, with all the brilliance of refracted light. Past lovers and friends are cast as remarkable characters, even the more minor ones such as Peter the undertaker "who prided himself on practical jokes, such as pulling up in his hearse next to a housewife stopped at a light and going 'Boo!'" With finesse, Henry exemplifies the complexity of intercultural marriage and racial issues through the disarming of the personal. And throughout, *Perspectives* is imbued with the keen observational, even just from a window: of a family picking through cast-out belongings from their burnt apartment, salvaging little more than a kettle. *Perspectives* can't help but inspire you to take note of your own refractions; singular moments that can dazzle with a lived-life universality."

— **Sandra Tyler,** author of
The Night Garden: of My Mother

FIRST EDITION, April 2026
LIBRARY OF CONGRESS CONTROL NUMBER: pending
ISBN 978-1-965784-58-7 HARDBACK
ISBN 978-1-965784-52-5 PAPERBACK
Printed in the United States of America, Canada, Australia,
Saudi Arabia, Japan, India, Brazil, and the European Union.

Book Design & Typography by **Kurt Lovelace**
Cover Art Raphael's *The School of Athens* (1509–1511)
Cover type *Bauhaus Dessau* **Alfarn** by Céline Hurka,
Elia Preuss, Flavia Zimbardi,
Hidetaka Yamasaki, and Luca Pellegrini.
Body & Chapter Titles set in **No 9T**
Headers in **Jenson** by Robert Slimbach
Flourishes set in Emigre Foundry **Dalliance**, by Frank Heine &
Emigre Foundry **ZeitGuys**, by Bob Aufuldish, Eric Donelan.
Typefaces licensed Adobe, Linotype, Emigre, & URW GmbH.

PierianSpringsPress.Com
PIERIAN SPRINGS PRESS, INC
30 N GOULD ST, STE 25398
SHERIDAN, WYOMING 82801-6317

CONTENTS

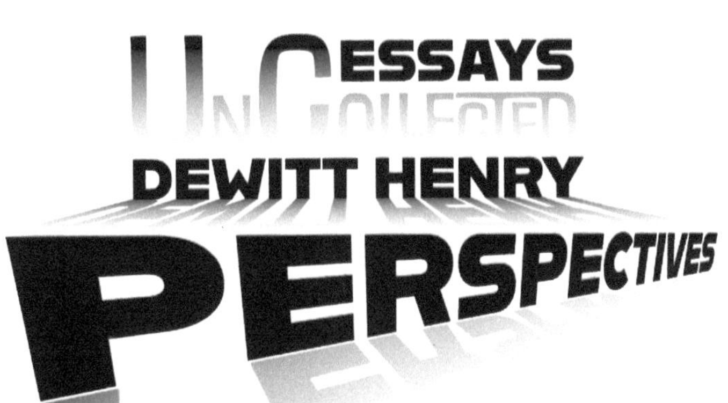

What If ?
Thoughts on Tille Olsen
First Love   Sever Hall   On Fact and Fiction
Face to Face   Memories of Henry Bromell
Remembering James Alan McPherson   The Saga of a Chair
Promises to Keep
UnCollected ESSAYS
DEWITT HENRY
PERSPECTIVES

PERSPECTIVES

I remember remembering. Remember, as I wrote in suburban Boston about my childhood in suburban Philadelphia, the gradual recovery of so much detail that when I stopped writing for the day, and walked to the grocery store, the sidewalk under my feet seemed unsubstantial, or at least seemed no more tangible, solid, or felt than my world had when I was eight. My physical surroundings and perceptions from then had all come back so overwhelmingly that they refused to recede.

❦ ❦ ❦

I know that there is a wholeness to the landscape in which I live. I know this as common sense, as experience, and by documentation and report. I live in Watertown, Mass., ten miles west of Boston, along the Charles River. I teach at Emerson College in downtown Boston, on the Common, and I commute there, mostly by car, along Storrow Drive, following the river the entire way. In warm weather I bike in occasionally. Here, I can show you on a map. Here is my landscape, my world, as seen from above. In fact I have an aerial photograph I tacked to my study's wall; the cover from a 1994 *Boston Globe* supplement about future planning, the photograph is exactly the same scale as the Boston area street map that I have tacked below it, both showing the Charles River meandering from Watertown, through Cambridge, into the Charles River basin, and then pinched through locks, into Boston harbor. My guess is that this is a view from 30,000 feet, too high to see cars, and higher than I have viewed this landscape while taking off from or circling to land at Logan Airport. The correspondence of photograph to map pleases me. I search for what I know. There among the crusty grid of downtown Boston, crusty because of the shadows cast by high-rise office buildings, is Boston Common. I can't see, but know, 180 Tremont, where I teach, just there, along the Common's lower right margin (for my last two years chairing the Writing Division, my tenth floor office windows overlooked the Common, where flocks of birds, pigeons probably, spread and spiraled, dipped and clustered like the process of my thoughts). And there, the rectilinear serrations of Back Bay, where years earlier from another office twelve floors up, I watched sailboats on the Charles River Basin and was distracted by rock music amplified from the half-shell on the Esplanade. The river loops north at what I know to be the Boston University bridge. Two full hand spans west from Boston Common, that green patch, mossy looking with treetops, is Mt. Auburn Cemetery, then more along the wavy ribbon of river, between what must be the Arsenal Street and North Beacon Street bridges, I see the red roofs of the Arsenal Mall. The river widens, creating an island that marks the local boat club, narrows at Watertown Square, goes north for what I know to be one mile, and there, that bridge marks Bridge Street, two blocks from my house. I think I can make out the square of Bemis playground across from us. My eye hungers, searching for purchase, for connection.

✻ ✻ ✻

I have lived in this landscape for 40 years, ever since graduating from college, one hundred miles west. My first glimpse came as I drove along Route 2 from Amherst for an interview at Harvard that spring. Just over a hill, the city skyline appeared suddenly and clearly in the distance. For years to follow, as I came and went from Harvard, finished my Ph.D. in English in 1971, lived in different Cambridge apartments and neighborhoods, from Harvard Square to Porter Square to Central Square to East Cambridge, before marrying and moving to Watertown, I would get as lost driving outside my neighborhood as if I had just materialized, say, in Atlanta, or Minneapolis, cities utterly unknown to me. Maps were no help. Attempting to return to Cambridge from a dance club or party in downtown Boston, I would end up somehow on the north shore, Chelsea, say, or Revere. I learned the city by getting lost. North, South, West. Shortly after I met Connie, who would become my wife, she got an emergency call at my Central Square apartment telling her that her father had just died in Florida; her married sister, Lonne, lived in Waltham, across from Brandeis, and would I drive her there? I had never driven out Mt. Auburn Street from Harvard Square, but with Connie choked and distraught beside me, and somehow reading directions from a paper in her lap, we headed past Mt. Auburn Hospital, then Mt. Auburn Cemetery, a dingy, over-traveled route with bus wires overhead and unused trolley tracks. I had no idea where I was going, or how much farther, but on the way I did count some seventeen funeral homes, each one a jolt in our faces, given Connie's grief, each for some other denomination or ethnicity, Armenian, Greek, Italian, Irish (given the names, O'Reilly, say, or Adrossinian). The drive seemed surreal, a pilgrimage of grief into unknown destinations. Eventually we reached an apartment complex across from Brandeis University, where all at once, I met most of this girl's family, sister, brother-in-law, niece, brother, brother-in-law's local parents and sisters, a sudden blur of intimacy and tribal embrace. Two years later, having lived together in two different Cambridge apartments, we were married at Connie's mother's home in Miami, Florida, surrounded by both our families; then with the idea of starting our own family, we found an inexpensive apartment out that same Mt. Auburn Street route, in Watertown. In contrast to the sordid singles world of Cambridge, Watertown seemed populated by working class, first and second-generation ethnic families. Shrines in front yards. Grape arbors. Laundry flapping in backyards, neighbors watching out for neighbors, village-style vegetable gardens. Our apartment was in the first floor of a two-family frame house, owned by Italian immigrants, who shouted "Mange! Mange!" through our ceiling, and who were cursed in English by their assimilated children. Mt. Auburn Street became my daily commute. The literary magazine, *Ploughshares*, which I had co-founded while I lived in Central Square, had already become my life, and its post office box in Central Square had to be emptied daily. I was teaching part-time now at Emerson, at Harvard, at Simmons, at Northeastern. My own father died in Philadelphia, just after we moved. Connie was pregnant. My widowed mother came to visit. Our daughter Ruth was born. Connie's water had broken, contractions begun, and I drove as fast and carefully as I could through traffic to the hospital near Simmons

College, having practiced the route for just this occasion. Two days after the birth, I drove Connie and the baby home. Twenty-one years later, to the day, my daughter has her first apartment across the grid of Boston, off Huntington Avenue, and after I find my way there to loan her our car for the birthday weekend, she is driving me back to Watertown, turning down Longwood to the Fenway, when I realize that we are retracing her first trip home.

⚜ ⚜ ⚜

Ten summers ago I felt displaced and devalued in my public life, and I had been trying to recover myself by mapping out my life, public and private, in memory and imagination. What was I doing here, now, as me? Who was "me"?

⚜ ⚜ ⚜

I had begun my fifties believing in my "self,"—even after the setbacks of secondary infertility in my marriage (which had been resolved by adoption of my son as an infant from Korea), and the rejection of my work as a writer. I had lost my father when I was thirty-five, my mother when I was forty-four. My two older brothers and older sister were scattered and distant: New Jersey, Colorado, Los Angeles. My closest friend, literary and personal, Richard Yates, died when I was fifty-one. I still believed that I was meant for recognition as a writer. I loved my family. I had built up *Ploughshares*, seeking to redress what I saw as the discouragement of literature in the marketplace, and had done so, lacking money, by relying on friendships, talent, resourcefulness and zeal.

In the heyday of the National Endowment of the Arts, one muckraking malcontent had even called me "the old grants baron." Beginning in 1984, I had found my first full-time job teaching at Emerson College. With some frustrations, things there had gone well, and I got tenure in 1989, became chair of the writing division, and negotiated the college's acquisition of *Ploughshares*. I felt that as chair I had made strides in hiring, in curriculum, and in enrollments. If there were soreheads in my fold, I had them well outnumbered in votes and in support from students and the administration, as well as in the world at large. But then a series of circumstances combined. The professor who had originally hired me, who had then stepped down as chair, elected to retire. My campus rival, an older man whose tenure I opposed in my chairperson role, managed to win sympathy across campus, was given tenure, and while active in the faculty union, wrote a new contract tailored to his personal situation and calling for faculty evaluation of chairs. Governance at the top of the college had gone berserk. An autocratic president was driven out; and after open war between the college trustees and the faculty, an insider faculty member had become president and needed the support of the faculty union. At this point, 5-4, my faculty voted against my renewal as chair, apparently inflamed by my rival. I couldn't believe that my friends, especially those that I had hired and supported for tenure, could turn on me, as coldly as strangers. I couldn't believe that I had so misread the terrain of interests and power in which I was located. I still can't, these long years later.

Once I was demoted, and one of these friends was put in as acting chair, I was also forced to surrender any real role in *Ploughshares* as my protégé took full control. As for my writing life, I had the support of an agent and had published a selection of best stories from *Ploughshares*, but my novel, which I had rewritten for a third time, along with a new second book, my family's biography, were rejected repeatedly, until the agent gave up.

⁂ ⁂ ⁂

Here is my driver's license description: age 58 male, white, 5 feet 10 inches height, 167 pounds weight, eyes green (glasses required), hair brown, thinning and graying. My fingerprints are on file, my dental records. Here is biology's map. Here is medicine's. Here are the microscopic reports of my infertility, say (16 million sperm per cc, 30 percent motility, 40 percent forward progression). Some day there may be the surprise of other microscopic reports of some part gone wrong, bringing closer the sentence of an ending. Not may be, will be. I know that.

In the spirit of Walt Whitman, I can sing my body electric, cataloguing its thoroughfares and provinces. Not biology's map, but imagination's, totemized fact. My eyes tour and swivel like cameras; some parts impossible to see, or rarely seen, craning in mirrors.

Eyes closed, felt: the rise of each breath, lungs full, the nostril sting of breathing in; then diaphragm and chest muscles contracting, exhale, again, again. Heart's pump.

I shower, I wash the body. I groom the body, shave, regarding in the mirror, the reassurance of reflection. How I look. My outside appearance. I touch my neck, my image shows the touch, but I feel the touch also. I close my eyes. I feel the touch.

The body hungers. Weakens, hungers. Desires. Aches. Sleeps, rises. Is ill, in pain. Is well. Floods with pleasure; pleases others. I take it for granted.

I dress the body.

I see myself in still photography, in movies, instant,

recent, long ago. I see myself in live video, there, on that TV, where I am used to seeing news and movies.

※ ※ ※

The oldest question of all: if you're not here, here in my daily life, proximate in Boston, MA, 1998, do you exist? You, reader, whom I have never met? You, my daughter, out of touch, first at Hampshire College, now in Guatemala on field study? You, my mother, dead since 1983? You, my father, dead since 1976? You, Richard Yates, dead since 1992? You, my sister Judy, in Pasadena; my oldest brother Jack in Colorado; my older brother Charles in New Jersey and now and then on a cruise on the Queen Mary II? My mother-in-law, Hazel, in Manhattan? My friend Jim McPherson in Iowa City? All structures of connectedness seem ephemeral, even my son today at school, my wife at school. What faith, what knowing or certainty can close these distances?

My mother in the last years, living alone in Philadelphia, used to say when we visited, "that the years fell away." We phone across space, speak our words in real time, with familiar voices. We write letters, we electronically mail thoughts and news in words. We send pictures. Very soon we will all have some form of videophones, and can watch each other and speak in real time no matter how distant on or off of this planet. We send audiotapes, videotapes for the keeping. Take family videos; capture family moments.

We are perhaps artists. We remember and imagine each other in episodes, in images, in memory loops. We embody our meaning—our disembodied selves—in art, in painting, music, stories. I teach Jim McPherson's stories and he comes all alive for me. I teach Richard Yates, and as Tim O'Brien has written (in "Lives of the

Dead"), being dead is "like being inside a book that nobody's reading"; as I read, Yates is all alive, his humor, his precision, his generous heart.

I think of when I was a teenager, my sister's empty room and those upstairs of my departed brothers, after each had left home for independent, adult lives. I would linger in their spaces, surrounded by their possessions and auras.

I live as if things don't matter, as if I don't feel, as if I don't long for lives lost and beyond interaction; but on the other side of numbness, I fear my howl of abandonment, my animal cry to emptiness.

❦ ❦ ❦

"DP's" they were called. "Displaced Persons." I was ten or eleven in those years between the end of World War II and the beginning of the Korean Conflict. They were Eastern European refugees walking in oddly misfitting and somehow foreign clothes and shoes along the back streets of Wayne and St. Davids, streets flanked by the houses and acres of suburban privilege. There must have been some charity relief organization that had found host families in our neighborhood to employ such refugees as maids, butlers, grounds people. Or perhaps the Valley Forge Military Academy, two miles away from my house down those back roads, was where they worked. I know the sight of them troubled me, their sense of being lost where I was found. A "DP" named Manfred had appeared in my sixth grade at Radnor Public School, circa 1952. When our town fire siren would sound at noon, our local custom, he would scramble to hide under a desk, because Manfred had been in real bombing raids. Also, he was obsessed with washing his hands in our deep arts sink in the back of the classroom, relishing the bar of Ivory soap as a luxury. Most of us, most of the class, rejected and mocked him as peculiar, except for the fattest girl in the class who took him over as her special project.

Some years later, as Castro took over Cuba, Cuban refugees began appearing. I remember my father hiring several in our family candy factory for menial labor and remarking that one of them had been a surgeon, but couldn't practice in America.

❧ ❧ ❧

E.M. Forster writes: "We cannot understand each other, except in a rough and ready way; we cannot reveal ourselves, even when we want to; what we call intimacy is only a makeshift; perfect knowledge is an illusion. [Fictional people] are people whose secret lives are visible or might be visible; we are people whose secret lives are invisible."

There are no secrets in art, because we agree that art is an act of imagination, an as if, rather than a literal experience with literal consequences. You paint your deepest emotions. I write myself to a place of open mystery. In real life, however, daily life—the life of compacts, trusts, reliabilities—stark frankness is wounding and offensive, denies necessary fictions (such as fatherhood, husband-hood, friendship, teacher-hood, citizenship, team person-ship), and in denying becomes itself a lie, a withholding.

This may be the basis of Catholic confession, and of prayer in general. If there is a God who knows everything, whose understanding is infinite and forgiving, then we are not alone. We believe in divine intimacy. We make or dream a space of utter vulnerability, beyond self-deceptions and working truths.

☙ ☙ ☙

Abused, forgetting becomes a power of pathology, a denial of life, a repression in psychological terms. I push myself away, estranged. Used correctly, I suppose, forgetting is "forget and forgive," though without remembering how do you forgive, and without forgiving, how do you forget?

☙ ☙ ☙

I have believed too readily that life is a quest for some absolute perspective, some final clarification. That adulthood itself is always that next horizon, that higher and wider perspective, from which everything becomes clear. That all experience, human experience, my experience, will overlap and coincide and I will be with the old men on Yeats's lapis lazuli, looking down on the spectacle of human folly and ignorance and futures and my glittering eyes will be gay.

I think of the perspectives of Zen. The idea of reincarnation, of one life-stage progressing in perspective to the next until one reaches Nirvana. I think of the "epiphany" in fiction as speaking for our faith in endings; of John Keats and his 24-year-old vision of "stepping towards truth."

But I don't know.

At the end, we see perhaps what we wished we saw, just as we do each night in dreams. Perhaps the quest for perspective is life's make-work. We search, we study, we dream. In small ways we acquire small wisdoms. And yet we forget more than we remember. In my own life how often I have willingly walked by hints and clues, and even by life's angels. I have chosen not to ask. Not to see. Not to know.

And then it comes. Your ending. It happens. Swiftly as fact. This is happening. Or slowly, and in pain, nine months, nine weeks. Your body claims your mind. Your body and your mind are one. Failing. Too tired to think, too weak.

Yes.

No.

Rosebud.

❧ ❧ ❧

Who *there* can remember, imagine or believe in *here*?

together along the benches Chuck had built, we lay down and stroked and kissed each other, until the first step of Mom, Dad or Jack on the stairs. After that summer apart we stopped dating and Ann started going steady with Rick Skillman. In mind and talk, boys were obsessed with the stages of getting to first (kiss), second (feel breasts), third (feel and finger vagina), and home (all the way), and girls seemed equally obsessed with limiting our progress. Ann was my first second.

From 9th grade on, I played the field without much success, dreaming, lusting, talking, but never really making out or getting romantic. Third and home would not come until my senior year, spring and summer 1959, with Kathie Ross, and love.

❧ ❧ ❧

"We're not rich," Chuck insisted frequently. "You and Judy think we're rich, but we're not. We're not even close."

"What are we then?" I asked.

"We're well-off. Well-to-do. We're comfortable."

Well-to-do I still found awkwardly better off than most of my Main Line Philadephia classmates, except for Billy Pew and Frank Scott, who transferred for senior year to our Radnor class from private schools, Haverford and George School. Pew's family was Sun Oil and Scott's was Scott Paper Products. Frank had his impact on Rudy Nottage, Weesy Mallinckrodt, Dave Bowman, and Pete Allen, to some extent. Weesy was one of the truly glamorous girls in the class, tall, with long blond hair. Rudy, Dave and Pete were in the Decades, along with Jim Anthony: our crooning rock quartet that actually had a recording made of "Silhouettes on the Shade" (side 1) and "Stagger Lee" (side 2), which was played by local

DJ's our senior year. Frank Scott, whose older brother Chuck had known and labelled "bad" at Haverford, lived a mile down Chamounix from our house. Frank's parents went to Europe our Senior summer and he turned their house into a non-stop party, where I stopped by, with Dave Bowman, only once. Frank fancied himself an artist. He had a motorcycle and would go roaring past our house, goggles on and Weesy, with her hair streaming, hanging on in back. He got the notion to sandblast a mural onto the long, unbroken wall of his family's living room and was working on it the time I visited, having taken down paintings, and moved and covered furniture. I heard later that his parents, horrified on their return, had to have the whole room re-plastered and painted. As a bearish, bushy-bearded, sandaled, jazz-digging bohemian, he had his following. Billy Pew, who went steady with Doerte, the German exchange student in our class, had a Christmas party and I remember feeling intensely awkward—I think we all did, his public school friends. It was in a stone mansion you approached up a long drive, where you were greeted at the door by a butler, and then were introduced to his stiffly smiling parents.

Judy Stradley's father, a lawyer and horticulturist, owned his own orchard off Sproul Road, some thirty acres or so, with a tractor and horses, which he stabled in an ancient barn with a hayloft.

Marion Watson's family had a big house back in the Ithan woods.

The majority of the college-bound, wasp, dating, party-giving and -frequenting kids were from medium income families with fair-sized houses. The Michels (lawyer), Galloways (minister), Teels (schoolteacher), Colburns (insurance agent), Kricks (real estate), Beesons (lawyer), Kings (doctor), Yerkes (pharmacist) and some others were members at St. Davids or Martin's. In North

Wayne, Howard Hopson, Ann Palmer, Rick Skillman, Barby Spillman: all lived in roomy Victorians. Others lived in smaller brick or stone bungalows, set among the larger houses on densely planted and tree-lined streets: Tucker Merrill, Fuvvie Bye; and still others in newer, modern houses, in developments, like Larry Arnold's, Liz Medica's, or Kathie Ross's.

Relatively poor included families living in two-family houses without yards, row-houses, or apartments, whose parents were blue-collar, and whose expectations were for trade, service, or business careers, rather than for college. This included mainly Italian kids and kids from cultivated black families; in the first instance, Joe Iacone, Franny Angelini, Jack Capelli, Paul DeSantis, Corky Cappola; in the second, Jim Anthony, Ethel and Margie Carroll, Diana Farmer, Claudette Johnson. It also included Paul Englebert, Joy Bennett, Harold Little, Neil Pine, and Dave Bowman.

Definitely poor included John Barnett, Earl Blackwell, George Holman. John's case I knew; those of others, I assumed, belonged to areas of town off-limits to me, such as Highland Avenue, towards Devon, or the black section behind St. Davids Golf Club, which Dad referred to categorically as "Henry Avenue."

I was aware, on dates, at parties, how parents looked at and placed me; where on the scale of social prospects I fit in. Mrs. Ross liked me; the Merrills liked me; the Davis's liked me. The Watsons could care.

Among our own ranks, the group that determined status was initially one of girls: Marion Watson, Sue Shellenburg, Ellen Bleecker. They decided on the boys, then had parties. There was a sorting out. You had to have a party to get invited to parties. You had to go the parties to have a girlfriend, or so it seemed to me. Of course there were equalizers. Sex and sports, as well as other intangibles, personality, say, a sense of humor, style, or a way with cars, were factors as important as money, or more so. Football and other sports, besides creating heroes for the girls, established grounds among the guys for camaraderie; and the girls, seeing how the guys admitted and admired another guy, would start to look at him with favor. Joe Iacone, for instance, bashful, gentle, our starting fullback, was dating Marion Watson for a while.

Dave Bowman and Judy Stradley were a cross-class romance; likewise, hard-working Dick Curley and Peggy Krick.

Dave was a victim of divorce, living with his mother and sisters in what must have been a cramped and embarrassing apartment. Neil Pine was the only other classmate I knew with divorced parents; but where Neil was edgy, a bully, and later transferred to another school, Dave was our class James Dean, whom he resembled in looks, as well as in his brooding, tragic manner. His father was an ad-man and playboy in New York, with an apartment in Greenwich Village, something like that, but whatever alimony he sent barely supported them. Dave's oldest sister had graduated years before, but his next, Joan, three classes older, had been head cheerleader, outshining even Holly Melcher. They all, including his mother (who, he has told me recently, was then having an affair with our married football coach, which caused a hushed scandel), were blessed and cursed by charm and good looks. In 11th grade English, our tough-minded, middle-aged teacher, Miss Rose Ferdinand, singled out Dave and me, and we became friendly rivals in our study of *Macbeth*, where we puzzled and argued about the concept of amorality, as opposed to immorality. Senior year, she had us debating whether the world owed us a living; Dave thought yes, I disagreed. I know I began writing seriously, and, for that matter, drawing and painting, which was our other talent in common, nearly as much to impress Dave as to impress Miss Ferdinand or the other kids, and I think he did likewise, both of us pushing towards some notion of the cool, a quality that was knowing, bold, and a little over our heads, and that concerned sex, love, God, and contempt for hypocrisy. But then besides art and writing, looks, a fair performance at football and track, a readiness to fight if challenged, a rapport with all kinds of kids, and a hip way of being first to catch or coin a witty expression or gesture—"Hey, g'om"—Dave also had the glamor of the Decades, where as lead singer, backed up by Pete Allen, Joe Iacone, Jim Anthony, and Rudy Nottage (also Paul Michel, sometimes, on drums), he held crowds spellbound, girls swooning. I envied him that popularity, and later his romance with Stradley, who resembled a thinner Natalie Wood.

Twelve out of 156 kids in my Radnor class were black. That included Diana Farmer, whose father was Dr. James Farmer, an official in the N.A.A.C.P, and Jim Anthony, our class president, who went steady with Claudette Johnson. It also included Earl Blackwell, slow-witted, good-natured, and sleepy, the first person brought to mind by the pop song, "Charlie Brown, he's a clown." As co-captain of the football team and center for basketball, Earl drew laughter for inevitably scratching his crotch while mumbling speeches into the pep-rally microphone. He ended up, immediately after graduation, as a sanitation worker.

Rudy Nottage was a special case. His friends were primarily white. In fifth grade, he used to walk Barby Spillman home because she lived around the corner, and partly he and I became friends because of my pursuit of her. His mother was a live-in domestic and his father the gardener for a rich family. He was one of the most popular kids in our class, respected for his humor, his generosity, and his brains. I remember the shock and outrage of everybody when Harold Little, who had been Rudy's best friend, lost his temper during a softball game in sixth grade and called him a nigger; whereupon Mr. Shock took Harold away for a long, searching talk, and afterwards Harold, who was a troubled kid, tearfully apologized, first to Rudy, then to all of us.

Rudy as a friend in sixth grade invited me to his house, which was the upstairs of the garage, a sizable outbuilding to the Victorian main house of what once had been an estate and now was a yard of three or four acres. I saw his room, though I did not meet his mother, and we mainly played outside. Then I wanted to invite him to my home, but Mom told me it would not be a good idea. Anna knew Rudy's mother from church. Mom did not directly forbid me to invite him over, but in her way, she did warn me, and I came to understand that I was not allowed to have black kids for visiting friends; that society, which meant the neighbors, frowned on it.

In high school, Rudy was class wit. He also was a starting half-back in football, from the pound teams all the way to varsity; a winning sprinter in track; and he played alto sax in Mr. Napier's twenty-piece swing band. Then he joined Dave and the others in the Decades. His yearbook entry says "...hopes for college."

At eighteen, the summer after graduation, mixed up with Scott and company, Rudy knocked up a girl from Henry Ave, and did the right thing by her, so the last I heard as I went to college, was that after his taste of the privileged class, he had been dragged under by circumstances, back into poverty, domestic life, and low horizons. I always spoke up for Rudy to Dad, as my friend, as someone I liked and admired. So it was with some satisfaction, axioms verified, that Dad sent me a local news article later on, after I had moved from college to graduate school. Rudy had walked into Avil's, the dry-cleaners, and shot the clerk there to death with a shotgun; he had been tried and sentenced for first degree murder and sent to prison. Drugs had been involved. I tried to imagine him, Rudy, fighting his domestic world, baby crying, married to a girl he did not love, hating his life and the menial job he needed to support it (he tried gardening I think), still in touch with the rich boys, who otherwise were no better or more gifted than he was, and thinking of their wild parties, and meanwhile the mid-sixties civil rights movement in the news, along with the protests against Viet Nam.

I try, but I can't imagine him. Not Rudy. Not murder. Not prison.

❧❧ ❧❧ ❧❧

Kathie Ross came to Radnor in 11th grade, transferring from Lower Merion, where she had gone for two or three years. They had lived in Puerto Rico for a while, then someplace in the South, before her father had gotten a job in Philadelphia. Her transfer to Radnor was the result of his promotion on that job, a new prosperity, and their buying a ranch house in a development off Sproul Road. But hardly had they moved, and had she started Radnor, when her father died suddenly of a heart attack. I had been aware of her before his death, but had never really known or dated her, so I never got to meet him. All along, she had been going steady with someone named "Ace" Townsend from Episcopal.

We met at Sally Yerkes' party, talked, slow-danced, drank punch or beer, and kissed. She liked me, without my trying to persuade her to, though she would put me through the ordeal of yearning, pleading, and of trying to win her from Ace, until she finally broke up with him. She was small-breasted, athletic, and wore her hair, light brown, in a page-boy. Her face was square-jawed and thin-lipped, but she was pretty in a tough way; and her tanned arms and legs were firm and beautiful. I was attracted to her combination of suburban good looks, madras shorts and all, her wit, her anger, and later, to her family pathos. She had a sister a year or so younger, Carol, and a brother four years younger, Johnnie. Mrs. Ross still had black hair, was slim, played golf, and gave and went to cocktail and bridge parties. Mr. Ross had been a Navy man at some point, and his portrait showed him in an officer's uniform. They became a family who welcomed and even seemed to me need me, as a fatherly man (I felt this), away from my family.

As for Kathie's anger: she warned me she could be a bitch, and that she was a bad sport; that when she played tennis for Lower Merion, she had thrown down her racket and walked off. That she was like that; she had no tolerance for frustration.

There was a hoody bravado about her, too, looking for kicks. Everything sexy and raw about dancing, she loved. The wildness, the drunken bachanal. I worried about her loyalty to me in the midst of that, and would get jealous when she slow-danced or flirted with Paul Michel, even while he was going steady with Marion Watson. A picture of Kathie and him, obviously bombed and hugging at a party, found its way into one of the yearbooks.

Another time, after we were going steady, after she had told me, "I love you, hon," and I would feel triumphant, superior, and normal, all at once, to be driving with her as my girl, and she would automati-cally sit in the middle, instead, as other girls had, edging purposely away to the passenger's door, and she would put her hand on and under my thigh, possessively. After I had that sense of belonging, which I had seen and envied others finding and enjoying, but never thought I could. After our petting had taken its progress. After we had parked. After I felt her breasts, and lower. After I had asked to feel her breasts inside, and had fumblingly unhooked my first bra. After we had kissed and kissed, especially in her driveway, so it steamed up the car, and Mrs. Ross would have to blink the garage light. After I told her about Dad's alcoholism, the first I had told anyone, girl or otherwise, as a way of sharing: then she had told me, as an equal revelation, about the family gardener in Puerto Rico— she had been brought up there, where her father was stationed, I guess—who, when she was eight or so, had shown her his penis, had had her play with it, and then had taken down her pants, fondled, and lain on top of her, but she had been too small and he couldn't make it go in, so he had ejaculated outside of her. She told me this in context, partly, of talking about her bad-girl appetite for sex, and for the illicit. And shocked, I told her I wanted to kill the man, over so many years. She said her father had felt that way too. But that the experience didn't seem so bad to her, the way it did to others; that she had liked and wanted it, in a way. Musing.

I exercised to have muscles, since Kathie told me that muscles were as exciting to girls as breasts were to boys. I worked my way from twenty to fifty to seventy-five push-ups. I started wearing a tank top to school, which Mom had bought me, no less, with no sleeves, in order to show my muscles off, and which drew frowns from some of the teachers, who had proudly marked me as college-bound and respectable. They didn't like the way Kathie and I walked, arms around each others' waists, in the halls, either. At some point, Mrs. Long took me aside and warned me not to let my reputation slip.

After sessions of heavy petting on dates, at parties and at her mother's house after school, sessions that included her letting me unhook her bra and feel her breasts and nipples, and finger her, and much dry humping, and sometimes in the steamed-up car in her driveway, her masturbating me until I came into a handkerchief: we'd actually made love for the first time, albeit by mutual accident. We had been in Dad's Ford station-wagon at the Main Line Drive In, kissing, with me sitting under her, and her straddling my lap, facing away from the movie screen, and my pants were off and my penis free and hard and instead of just rubbing it on her panties and against her vulva, I pulled her panties down under her dress (no one outside could see) and around her buttocks as much we could, and then was rubbing my penis against her wetness and hair, and then the impulse just to work it in a little way became irresistible and her motion too, so I slipped in all the way, deep inside her, hot and wet, and unimagined by any approximations, along with the awareness and elation of what we'd done, that we were fucking, and first time for both of us, and no tearing of a hymen or anything painful or bloody for her. I was able to thrust several times, enough to be really doing it—this fearful, astonishing and irreversible act—before I felt on the verge of coming and pulled out. And for then that was enough. The threshold was crossed for us. We loved each other.

Soon after that first time, early in June and after graduation, we plotted that Kathie would come over to my house when Mom was away, a certain day. I was to call her. The day, when it came, was tense and abrasive; I was restless with Mom to be gone, then called Kathie and her mother hadn't brought back their car yet, and the afternoon was passing. On the surface, we kept things innocent, she was just to come over, nothing more than that, so we could be together and I could share my home life with her, show her the house. But there was deliberate stealth to it. Mom wasn't to know. All along there was some fear that Mom would not approve of her, on any grounds; whereas Mrs. Ross openly welcomed me. Kathie had to come before Mom came back, and the longer our plan was frustrated the more irritable, cold and impatient we became to each other on the phone. But then at last she called and was coming, though it was late. And then she arrived, parking her station-wagon right out front.

What happened then was not entirely innocent or spontaneous. I had been impressed by a scene in *Some Came Running* by James Jones, where the teenage writer sneaks his girlfriend home and makes love to her on his childhood's bed. Excitedly, I showed Kathie around. We went down to the cellar and I showed her my print shop, and this was important to me, to be showing her my most personal and private world, and I kissed her down there, against my type-cases, and then we went up to see my bedroom, where she looked over my writing desk and stuff on the walls (it was a humid, sticky afternoon, too), and after hollow preliminaries, like nothing was intended except one friend looking over another's room and books, we started kissing and making out in some awkward, semi-stoop on the floor. Then I had her blouse off, and half-lifted, half-urged her onto my bed, and had my shoes and pants off and penis free. She didn't want to take her bra off, because she was afraid of Mom coming home, something like that. And with no more sophisticated idea than to repeat and embellish on our drive-in experience, I was in her, on top of her, for real, three, five, six strokes, when I felt myself coming and pulled out, to catch most of my ejaculate in my palm. I got up and hurried to the bathroom, to wipe my hands and flush the evidence, then wash myself, and when I came back to Kathie, we did, in fact, hear Mom's car in the driveway.

Kathie groped for and pulled on panties, then bermudas, shrugged into and buttoned her blouse. Me too, my underpants, pants and shirt. Heart pounding, I felt fatalistic: just here it comes, and no escape. But Kathie hurried down the front stairs, out the front door, and managed to drive off, just as I clambered down the back stairs to greet Mom, who came in the kitchen door with packages.

Here, I confess, memory fails, but she must have been puzzled and suspicious. "Whose car was that? Wasn't that Kathie I saw? Why couldn't she stay?" I must have lied and Mom must have let me lie. Did I say it was someone else? Judy Stradley, for instance, and that she'd just been passing and stopped to say hello, but was late getting home? Or that it was Kathie, and she'd only stopped for a minute, and was late. "Well, she should at least have stayed to say hello. Didn't you hear me coming in? I don't like that." Whatever Mom permitted me, she didn't like, but she didn't cross-examine me or force the issue, either.

A day or so afterwards, Kathie left with her family for eight weeks at their summer resort on Squirrel Island, off the coast of Maine. We'd talked about my coming up to visit. We'd also worried whether I had pulled out in time, whether any sperm had been inside, whether she might get pregnant. And for the next two weeks, hearing nothing, I wrote her everyday. I holed up in our basement playroom, where it was cool, and where, with Chuck's old typewriter, I had set out to write a novel over the summer. In my letters I kept asking, emphatically, how she was, assuming that she would know what I meant. I was living through the real possibility of disgrace, of not going to college. I prayed to God to help. To forgive me. To make it be all right. If such a small slip as that, such a natural, good, necessary thing could result in ruined lives, then where was justice? I thought of Mom and Dad, how they would react. I was too young to be married, too young to have a baby, to have life's responsibilities close down around me.

Kathie, meanwhile, promised not to mess around, but then went on to write about her high times messing around, and wanting to know about mine. "All the boys up here are either older or younger than I am...I miss you terribly....I just want you to know I could never do anything up here or any other time that I might be separated from you or that I would be afraid or ashamed to tell you about....Last night I had a blast...I wish I could write you letters as good as you write me, but you know I'm no writer. Be assured I feel the same things you do." Finally, in early July, I sent her a telegram: "Are you okay?" and got back a special delivery letter, she was, "You haven't done anything wrong. I love you. How's that?....Everybody is kidding me about your daily letters, but I love it and they can't wait to see you...Well, just one more thing....DON'T WORRY!!"

Relief. Hosannahs. She told me later, she'd been amused at how upset I'd gotten. She hadn't even thought about it.

We continued to look forward to my visit. I poured out my heart in letters with no self-consciousness about cliches: "When I get to Squirrel Island, my love, we will lie on pine needles in the shadows of the forest floor." She wrote back: "Two more weeks and you'll be here. I'm so excited. Please let me know what day, and how you're coming."

Days, I swam, played golf, or both, then closed myself

in the cool of the basement and wrote away. Besides letters, I was writing my "novel." Called "Search for Stone," where "stone" meant something fixed, true, and certain, it concerned a younger boy, whose loneliness and whose search for meaning apart from the hollow, self-congratulating world of his parents, resembled mine; it also resembled the boy's in Ray Bradbury's *Dandelion Wine*, which I'd been reading. My boy was drifting towards self-damage, if not suicide, but then I wanted him to recognize his value and to take responsibility for himself.

Mom and Dad had hedged all along about the Squirrel Island idea, and I had been embarrassed to ask, but now they flatly refused to let me go. No arguments. Why not? But I promised! Mrs. Ross thinks I'm coming! No. It's not proper, Mom said. You're too young. If you were getting married, that's the kind of thing you'd do. Mrs. Ross just isn't thinking. She's more lenient or permissive about these things than we are. Sorry.

This was their power play, as parents, and I had to write Kathie, sorry, but my parents wouldn't let me.

From then on things were never the same. A choice had been made. When Kathie came back, in August, she had already turned her mind to the new life at Duke, a life without me, as I went on to Amherst College. We saw each other, and I wrote her in an unsent letter: "You have been losing hold day by day until you can't even accept me as a friend. I'm sorry about the sex we have shared since you have been back, for your part it was without love, for mine it was a last desperate attempt to keep some sign that you still liked me....I have found faith in something, and knowing how hard it is for me to do that, you must also know it is impossible for me to lose that faith now. I found faith in you...You have a lot of things influencing you right now, college, the freedom you want, but I think there is something for both of us that will eventually reach through all that, and that you will come back, we will come back."

❧ ❧ ❧

At boys-only Amherst, while other freshman sought dates from nearby Smith and Mt. Holyoke, I felt worldly and sufficient to have had my adult romance, tantamount to marriage, and to have my girl from home, whose picture I kept on my desk, and to whom I wrote constantly.

Despite her letters back, however, protesting loneliness for me and a wish to be married rather than go on with the work of college, she was dating; and in particular dating an upperclassman—as she wrote to me that September: "I finally accepted a blind date offered me by my sophomore advisor. I honestly had so much fun! Larry is 24, a Junior here, and has been in the Navy for two years." Neither Thanksgiving nor Christmas vacations worked out as reunions. She skipped Christmas at home and wrote me in January that "if Larry ever does leave you can pick up the pieces if you'll still be around, because there will be pieces." They were pinned by March, married in April, though I didn't get the news until July.

As I began my sophomore year, she was separated, living home, and I had visited her there, captivated by the baby girl, which I helped to bathe and powder. Her mother out, baby asleep, we started to make out. Her ambivalence continued. She wrote to me at school. Larry lived in Kingston, N.C. She told him that if he came to visit at her mother's, she'd rather he slept in the guest room than with her. But then changed her mind: she wanted more than anything to go back to Larry and never leave again. "We might have married if I had for waited for you," she wrote me, "however, we too would have had some bad times and I would have left you a couple of times too." But immediately she changed again: "I don't think I know what love is."

She saw a counselor, hoping to save the marriage. I took off a special weekend in mid-October and traveled home to see her. She had just come back from Kingston, where Larry had refused to consider getting back together until hunting season closed.

This time, baby asleep, and her mother out again, we talked and drank in their living room and ended up making love on the couch. I used a condom for the first time, having learned this much from my fraternity brothers, but when we finished, the condom had slipped off inside her. A week later, she wrote to me back at Amherst, "It is my turn now to worry about being pregnant. I couldn't go back to Larry because it wouldn't be his baby (he knows that we haven't had intercourse for months). I couldn't marry you because I am not divorced. It would take me about a year to get a divorce. I couldn't go to school because I'd have another baby to take care of."

I don't recall my response. I was popular suddenly at Amherst, dating a Mt. Holyoke girl, involved in fraternity life, and absorbed by my classes, editing the college literary magazine, and my writing. If briefly I had ever thought of marrying her with Larry's baby, by now I had had second thoughts, and probably would have argued for an abortion. But soon she wrote (again) that the pregnancy had been a false alarm, and that she had learned a lesson. "'Thou shalt not commit adultery,' and that is exactly what we were doing."

We didn't write again. She and Larry reconciled and moved on in life.

Mom and Mrs. Ross would from time to time meet and talk in the supermarket or at the golf club and I heard later from Mom that Kathie had been divorced, then remarried; then, I think, divorced again.

Nine years later, our twenties spent, Kathie called me at graduate school in Cambridge. I didn't recognize her southern accent. She told me, searchingly, hopefully, that she was living with her two children in Tennessee, but I only responded with commonplaces. Nothing personal to share.

SEVER HALL

(1963)

A. You are a young woman, twenty-three, perhaps,
    a graduate student at Harvard in anything but
    English. You do not take courses in Sever Hall,
    on the North side of campus. But you are
    taking a Ph.D. in the History of Art, perhaps,
    and as you cross from your studio course in
    Carpenter Center, hurrying to the library, 8:45
    a.m. perhaps, you take a path past one side of
    Sever, where there is a fire escape door. The day
    is bright, clear, and cold, exhilarating, and just
    as you are passing you hear the door bang
    open, and you turn, surprised, to see a young
    man, younger than you, no coat, spewing
    vomiting—arghh!—over the railing. Your eyes
    meet. You burst out laughing uncontrollably.
    You've never liked literature either.

B. I've come to Harvard from Amherst. I live
    several blocks away, in a seedy rooming house,
    where I share a bathroom and kitchenette with
    ten or so other roomers, and my landlord is a

maharishi. That first fall I am in a discussion course in 17th Century Prose taught by Anne Ferry, my first woman teacher since high school. I love her intellect. I love the way she reads out loud, making anything beautiful. I tell her, after she has read a passage from John Donne, John Milton, or Sir Thomas Browne, that she could read just as beautifully from the telephone book, that the beauty is in her intonation, her savor of voice and of words, as much as it is in the art of the prose. As a fiction writer, I claim my own authority in the art of prose, my own intuition of verbal style and music. And I will admit also, though she presents such a professional air, eyeglasses, slightly graying hair pinned back yet frizzy, I find her deeply feminine and sexy. She is I am guessing five or six years older than I and she is married to a man older than she, a poet and Wordsworth expert, who also teaches here. Probably she was his student. Somehow, I feel, we flirt. I work my hardest for her and she gives me A's. I am taking three other classes as well. A lecture course on 19th century American Literature; another on Samuel Johnson; another on the 18th Century Novel: all in Sever Hall, different rooms, days, and hours. I like to think I am her star. That morning, we are reading Sir Thomas Browne's "Religio Medici," and I have rushed breakfast somehow, eggs, bacon, and toast, up early having studied late into the night; I know I am rushed. I get there. I am in class, closed in by a row of chairs. We are bending minds to the task, the sentences, the words. She is asking me questions. I begin to feel clammy, cold sweats. What is it, I wonder, that causes me to imagine being nauseous? The notion, the fear, seems to precede or to presage the event; has before: not may, but will this time, always will, uncertain certainty. The clammy forehead, shakes. The struggle, no, I'm not. Not now, not here. I'm just imagining. But then the dizziness, the growing fact. Biting my lip. Swallowing saliva, again, again. We are discussing Sir Thomas Browne, that great amphibian, his rolling periods. She looks with annoyance and alarm, as I stammer, "Excuse me, I have to leave!" I push to my feet, and the class's eyes on me, querulous and amused, as I leave my notebook and books behind, and, horrified, make for the classroom door, and as, maturely, Anne Ferry allows for my adult judgment and continues with the class. I feel the convulsion in my stomach and the first taste of sour burning, my stomach's gorge, now, my god! mouth filling, lips clamped, hands over my mouth. I rush for the exit down the hall, spewing helplessly— between my fingers actually, cheeks puffed like Dizzy Gillespie's—a little on the landing, then bursting out the fire door, bang! outside, steps, a railing, and letting all go, first choke, second, more, over and over, spewing, choking in the frigid air, and no more than ten or fifteen yards away, on the path, is this girl, this witness, startled by the sight, eyes meeting, and she's laughing. So am I, until I weep. She keeps on going. I do too, the sickness purged, like that.

C. Who was that girl, I wonder 57 years later as I read through my notebooks. Who did she become, or not? How was her life? As for Anne Ferry, I loved her books on Milton's epic voice (1983) and on Renaissance anthologies (2002). She went on from Harvard to tenure at Boston College. I had no idea of her passing in 2006, until just weeks ago I heard David Ferry, now 94, read his poem, "Some Things I Said," with its plaintive line, "Where are you, Anne?"

CAMBRIDGE VIGNETTES

(FROM THE SIXTIES)

I.

S he came to me late the other night-after I'd forgotten her and was busy working on something. About midnight, I guess. She was in her red robe—and I was civil, but preoccupied. I wanted none of her. But also that day I had just finished *The Story of O.*, and my mind was full of sadistic whimsies and the mood of anythingness that the book instills: the pound of fleshness. Anyway, I sneered at her and told her she bored me, and satirically, that she was a mass of mediocrity. And she said she was on her way to take a shower, but she had a boil on her behind, and what did my medical book say about that?

She was lying on my bed. And this was funny, so I got out Dr.Spock and read her about boils in there—salt water compresses. And then I dug out the Anglo-Saxon charm against wens, and recited it ritualistically to her unwilling, uninterested ears:

Wen; wen, little wen ...
Shrivel as coal on the hearth,

Shrink as muck on the wall,
And waste away like water in a bucket.
Become as small as a grain of linseed ...
And become even so small
that thou become naught ..
(Wenne, wenne, . wenchichenne, ...
Clinge pu . alswa colon heorpe,
scring pu : alswa scerne awage, ...
litel pu gewurbe pet peu nawiht gewurbe.)

And I asked her if it felt better-and she answered, No, but now her ears hurt. And I got up to put my book away and said I didn't care, I enjoyed reading it, for my own sake. And what I thought was funny, was that even Anglo-Saxons had wens, probably from eating too many spices and drinking too much ale. And I sat down beside her and jokingly ran my hand up her leg, towards her ass. And she recoiled, "Hey!" "Um," I pondered, "nothing on underneath?" I tubbed her tail and back. And I forget what next. Except that I wasn't particularly interested in having her there—didn't desire her. And there were, as she shifted position, little exposures and glimpses of her breasts. But I wasn't interested. And I started kidding about masochism and pulled a large wooden club from underneath the bed, and started hitting my head with it. To her, NO! Don't!

Oh—and then we decided on salt treatment of the wen. She hiked up her robe to show it to me, on the white globe of the round of her ass, this bright red spot. And was I supposed to squeeze it? I peered at it closely, like a doctor—and disinterested. And said I'd go get some salt water. So I did and came back and got a piece of cotton and dabbed it and covered it with a band aid. So much for the wen.

Then I guess with mock roughness to her mock resistance and protest I parted the front of her robe and pulled it down over her shoulders, exposing her breasts—which still didn't especially matter, though they were pretty. And I brushed them upwards with my fingers and palms, and kissed them. And then I had my ballpoint pen in my pocket and I had an impulse–so I took it out. What are you doing? she insisted. What are you going to do? I had in mind that scene in "0." where Sir Stephan brands her ass with his initials; ironically. And I started to draw on her right breast—to her bewildered amusement—a round eye to the right of the nipple and another to the left and then a grinning mouth under the nipple, with a Cheshire cat grin, one tooth missing. And the nipple was a perfect nose. So then I got her a mirror and bobbled it for her-and the effect was irresistibly hilarious. "I could make a living at this, you know. They pay money at the Lido for less ... in Paris." And she said as how I was outrageous. And would I do something with the other one? So I made that the face of tragedy, gloomy and weeping and a drop falling from the funny red nose. And then I bobbled them back and forth. And on her leg I drew an arrow pointing North. And then the footprints of a leprechaun returning to the womb, and then on her other leg the semblance of several tiny little crabs.

And she said, Oh, no! And wriggled back, shedding the robe entirely until she made a sort of calendar tableau. The robe was red and spread out under her and against the wall—she was leaning back to the wall and her legs off to one side and the lamp on my telephone table was casting light down on her from the side. And I said she looked like a stamp. What kind of stamp, said she. Some Italian stamp ... Titian, I said. And I admired her, a definitive nude. And me sitting on the large bed, just in front of her, fully clothed. And what was amusing was I still did not particularly care for sex–in fact the whole business would be too involved for my mood now—too much trouble and effort. And I was thinking that as I admired her for simply being a picture: for being a classical study in the nude who aroused a dim aesthetic interest, but no sex. And then I started to take a detached interest in her body, peering through her pubic hair for anything that looked like crabs. At the root of each hair. And she helped and said she'd already given a good look and didn't find anything. And I thought to myself, a la Henry Miller, what a funny-looking thing a cunt is. The slightly discolored-tannish flesh of its lips and, on her anyway, the double fold at the ventral tip. And then I kissed her stomach and started to move lower with my kisses, but she said, No, don't! And so my hand did, probing between the lips and happening onto a substantial clitoris.

I was feeling mean and anything goes and enjoying it, and I was curious ... to see what she would be like in this kind of pleasure. And caressed her there until she twisted and moaned and reached down, saying, No. Stop! Stop! but still the thrills going through her and she pushed my hand on down into her vagina, getting me excited now too, with her excitement. And she spread her legs and writhed and I pressed my face against her stomach as I kept probing and circling with my fingers up against the round bump of her cervix (is it called?) and going in and out while she was in the first real orgasm-ecstasy I've gotten out of her.

And finally she was spent and convinced me so and we lay still a moment. Then: Oh, I could kill you! Why did you de that? And I chuckled, because you wanted me to. And she said, I know, but I could kill you. I haven't done that for five years! (disgusted with herself). And she got up and wrapped her robe close around her and went to sit in the chair, picking at her toenails, and scowling up at me. What's the matter, I said. That's one way of having pleasure, and the pleasure for me is in giving the pleasure to you. And she said, I don't know. And I said, Maybe you don't like it because I didn't do anything you need a man for. Or another person even, if you want to be realistic. That's right, she mused. Heidi could have done that. And then she got up: I could kill you for... being so alive, she said,—much to my gratification, although I couldn't quite follow her reasoning. Except that she struck me as very dead. Then she left me to take her shower; slept down there.

I guess that's the last time we had anything like sex together.

II.

I had a cigar and a beer and was sitting there thinking my thoughts and eating free hors d'oeuvres when along comes this professorial, flat-faced, thickly bespectacled intellectual sort, sits next to me. Okay. It's a crowded bar. And after a while he makes a remark to me—about Charley's Kitchen being the only good bar in Cambridge. And I say, sure, especially if you're starving and like free hors d'oeuvres. He says, they're good. And everything here is good and cheap. Just making conversation, you know. Like any barfly loner. We talk about relative merits of Cambridge bars, and his Cambridge life goes back about twenty years the way he talks. I said this looked like it was shopkeepers and mailmen, then Whitey's up to Boylston for a slightly rougher crowd, and finally the Harvard Gardens where they all said Fuck and spat on the floor. And in his bespectacled, goggled way he says he doesn't especially mind the first (saying Fuck) but he does the second. He's about forty, I'd guess, and authentically intelligent and learned, so I'm flattered to interest him, see? (And he had a bare-toothed, buck-teeth grin.) We talked about politics and then about backgrounds. What did I do? Seriously? And I told him. And he said I had a fine sense of humor, a sharp tongue, young man. And he was looking for a booth, then, because he wanted to order a hamburger and finally we got a booth, and did I want a hamburger? I said no, and got some more hors d 'oeuvres. And paid for the next round of beers, since I don't like being bought for. And we went on to talk about ourselves—and mostly to my gratification, me—but played Where Was He From—which turned out (he said) to be Indiana. And, as I said, his field was teaching or whatever in political history. And he said he was writing a book. And the next move was, as we were set to depart-me to home and dinner-to relieve ourselves of all the beer. So he leads the way to the men's room. And there I do have suspicions, only because if a guy so friendly is queer, surely as you are pissing together there would be some indication. But no. I only remember feeling embarrassed pissing with him, urinal to urinal, which may be indication enough. And then out on the street. I have the buzz of a drunk going, and he asks it seems in the same spirit whether I won't come to his place for more to drink? Rather insistent. Which seems too insistent. Which seems too insistent for drinking buddies, but still not definitely wrong, really, except as I thought in my own depraved and overly suspicious mind. Anyhow I declined. Upon which we exchanged names. His was Mark Reynolds, which I take to be an alias or code name. And he then asked could he come to my place? While I ate? And this was the crucial stupidity if there was one. Because I shrugged and said (feeling a little awkwardly forced), sure. And he wanted to take a cab, but I said don't be ridiculous. And we walked, still talking a blue streak about nice abstract, intellectual type things. And we get to 50 Irving and my room. I guess I was operating on the sentiment that the guy was lonely this afternoon and genuinely impressed by me and the flaw was my own vanitas in that respect. For once he was here-in my privacy, you see, I had to play the Great White Host. And asked if he wanted any of the stew I was reheating? No. Well, I only had coffee to offer him to drink, would he have some of that? All very formal and courteous, see, as I would be to one of my professors, or even to one of my formal, conversational friends. And he would have coffee—so I leave him and go down to fix the coffees and my own dinner in the kitchen. After ten or fifteen minutes I return, with cups and my stew bowl, to find him sitting on the floor in front of my bookcase. Okay, I would do the same, perhaps. Only he's losing some of my regard as an idea man; the conversation is getting hollow; he's acting more and more like an intellectual phony. Forcing conversation and blatantly ingratiating me. So I give him his coffee, and a slice of rye bread, and commence to eat. And put, apropos of his observations about the same, some records on. He had remarked on a Shubert record I had out-Oh, you like Shubert! I said, No, it was Carol's record—the Carol whom I had made a special point of telling him back in the bar I was going with and expecting to meet for dinner. And he asked me several times, well where is she? When is she coming? ... carefully remembering her name. And I said my own favorites were Beethoven, Sibelius and Bartok, whatever that meant, and did he have any objections? Ah! Beethoven, he says. So I put on Beethoven. And he asks again about Carol, where is she? To which I reply, I dunno. Coming soon, I hope. (She didn't). So now he sits in the green circle chair by the window, until I toss an ashtray to him on the bed, and he moves a little awkwardly close to sit on the bed, while I'm sitting near it at my desk,and the dish of stew in my lap. And he responds to the music pensively and emotional-histrioni-cally-as a professorial sort should. Tells me about Beethoven's life and I should read the moving biography by Sullivan. And tells me how the Pastoral Symphony was the first record he ever bought. Etc. And I rejoin with similarly maudlin stuff'; which he indulges. And he asked if I read Plato (having seen several volumes in my book-case), and I said yes (forgetting Alcibiades). And then he went from Plato to Nietsche. Who was his mentor and idol in philosophy. As the anti-Plato. And here he began to sound a bit obsessive and off-kilter. Because mature, balanced folks I know—it seems—know better than to think of Nietsche as the sublime refutation of Plato and the True Message for the Present Day. But who am I to argue? And also he swooned over Dostoyevski, to my defense of Tolstoy; and sympathized, in Renaissance jargon, with the beasts more than. the angels. While I said I was the other way. And Ayn Rand, which somehow follows. And Thomas Wolfe. Okay, that sort of chatter. And I got what I deserved for being susceptible to it. For very next thing, soon as I'd finished eating and he was sitting, leaning on the bed, I said, ahem, look, I'd like to get some work done tonight and he said I can tell when I've worn out my welcome, and I have. And no, I said, no offense. I intend to work is all. Look, give me your number– see—and we have parties or something. I'll give you a call. You'll really call? he asks. I can't promise that, says I, but maybe. So he gives me a number. And stands up, smoking a cigarette. And boggles, awkwardly close, like he's forgotten something. And I hold up the ashtray for him, embarrassed and perplexed. And he-then-leans suddenly close and kisses me on the ear.

Well, that, anyway, resolved the doubt. Oh, NO-buddy—says I—rather like a fluttery young thing, not wanting to offend him, yet not wanting any of that; I am very heterosexual, got it? Are you really? he asks, as if he knows better. I am, says I, and very satisfied with the arrangement. What, just lonely then? And I explained, No, but I responded to loneliness. Well, I never force anything, he says, smiling and resigned. But just a little goodnight kiss? And I put up my hand between us. N-O! None of that. Come on. Cut it. You're sure? he asks. I AM. Okay, he says, and with urbane grace departs—gone.

III.

The building I watch every day, out my window: a brick apartment building, whose windows have caught my voyeuring curiosity enough so I know the folks who live there—suddenly this noon billowed smoke and burst into fire. Fire-fighting equipment, etc. was slow coming, and pretty soon flames were coming put the roof and windows—I saw them eat up curtains and then windows pop! And a woman was shrieking hysterically for her child: enough to sicken me, watching. I learned it was the child later—who had escaped. But all I knew was this inhuman shrieking at the time-and the first firemen unconcerned or helpless to locate or do anything about it. It might have been someone trapped and burning alive, but I didn't want to know. I wanted to accept it as a matter of course and forget it. Unnerving sounds. And all the apartments familiar to my eye, without occupants, were flaming now. Then fire trucks arrived and men got organized, but so slowly. And all this in an emergency snow hazard too, in the midst of the storm and bitter cold. The fireplug near which my car was parked was frozen. They couldn't get any water. And then they had

FIRST LOVE

A MEMOIR

By 1957, when I got my driver's license and had the use of either Mom's Buick, or more likely, Dad's station wagon, a lot of my theater movie-going was transferred to either the Main Line Drive-in, in Devon, or the Exton, farther west, summer and winter both. Prior to that, non-movie dating had been restricted to parties. My little black books for ages 13 and 14 have me going frequently to Mrs. Hill's dances, to a swimming party, with a date to "The Barefoot Contessa," a school dance, a dinner party at Clark Colburn's, movies, then more and more parties, though there were some I would hear of beforehand, hope wretchedly to be asked to, and then come to realize that I was pointedly not to be asked.

Ann Palmer, new to Radnor, blonde, intelligent, was the first girl to really like me back, however briefly. We dated in the spring of 1955—the spring of my sister Judy's marriage, of my 8th grade, and of my brother Chuck's tour in the army—and she was partly the reason for my having my own first party that June 11 ("pick up Ann, 7:45"). We made out at these parties, and this time, dancing first in the dark, as other couples slouched or lay special trucks draw hose from hydrants on other blocks and finally got a stream directed towards the window where the flame was showing. And from then on it was a fight for control, about two hours of smoke and cold and several firemen smoked out and carried away: and smashing windows and working their way up and into the top floor apartment and onto the roof. It was in the top apartment where it first broke out, to my eye at least. But rumor has it, and the efforts of firemen later indicate, that the heart of the fire was in the basement: that the furnace exploded or something and either flames went up the heating ducts or up between the walls or something. All that destroyed. Those young couples, especially the husbands returning from class or work and nothing there, but now the fire's out, a charred brick shell. Not something you can believe happening. Their belongings, everything, gone. The terror is self-interest, of course (what if this firetrap went?). Coming home and finding this place charred, my books, papers, etc. Where do people go next? Having this descend upon them, arbitrarily. In the midst of their lives suddenly staggered. I can imagine them looking at me now, or the likes of me, going on in my ordinary life, worrying about literature and shopping and my car...and pitying me. And on my side, the queer, helpless sense of guilt in being untouched and still in the midst of my life, as I pass by one of the burned-out wives who lived over there, and who is grouped with some friends warming themselves in our foyer .... I remember seeing the woman in the top apartment looking out her window this morning, an hour or so before the fire: looking out, as I was, at the snow.

※ ※ ※

The following day is clear and the gutted shell of the building there, an object of speculation to occasional passersby, but otherwise quite simple. Covered with snow. And the couple who lived in the top apartment, with four kids and a large Labrador retriever come to pick through the snow-covered heap of charred debris that the firemen have thrown down. The dog snaps and chases too much and the father lashes out at the oldest boy, Matthew, and tells him to take the dog home and keep him there (wherever that may be). The mother picks around nervously here and there, shakes out a frozen skirt. The father finds the kid a box with a radio in it that doesn't look too damaged. The mother has a brown paper bag with her that she is gradually filling with whatever there is—pots and pans and bits and scraps-whatever didn't bum. And meanwhile some firemen have come back and gone into the building, informing a rude, nosy old woman who is gawking after them, that they're only after some tools they'd lost. And the old woman remains to pester the burned-out family with the obvious questions, until the mother turns on her with exasperation and shouts: "I don't want to talk to you. Go away and leave us alone!" And then these two snow-shovelers aged thirty or so, pass by, without seeing or noticing the family, and one of them pauses to look over the fence at another pile of debris fromwhich he extracts a metal towel rack. And he obviously sees a chance here for some good scavenging. He stops the firemen on their way out and asks them some questions. And then with a whetted interest (his buddy shows none), but still some uncertainty, not scrupling to check a shoe he finds on the sidewalk and reject it, he watched the father working on the pile of trash round the back of the building. And then, finally, he hangs around the mother and kids and her paper bag and picks up the kid's radio, as if it were unclaimed, to examine it. And this elicits sharp words from the mother and no doubt a rejoinder from him, to which she loudly replies: "Look, 1 live here!" After which, with his towel rack as his prize, he moves reluctantly on by. Then the family leave too, with their first load, the paper bag, the kid with his radio, the father with a frame of a chair over his back, and a kettle.

MY OWN PRIVATE CAMBRIDGE

After several heartbreaks in my mid-twenties, lessons in a sentimental education that overlapped with my studies in graduate school, I resolved never again "to lose my head over a piece of tail," as a worldlier fraternity brother once had put it. I was preparing to retake my Ph.D. orals and then to begin my dissertation on *Romeo and Juliet* at Harvard, while also teaching freshman composition, and working on my first novel. I would find girls, I told myself, who were users willing to be used. To be stylish for my last woman, distraction over whom had caused me to fail my orals in the first place, I had let my hair grow and bought, as a joke, a pair of striped bell-bottoms. The cultural backdrop, meanwhile, had changed from hippy carnival to the worst of the Johnson years, student protests, the Manson murders, riots, daily Viet Nam kill reports, draft lotteries. Nixon was elected.

A twenty-two year old secretary named Vicki had moved into my Cambridge rooming house. She was pretty enough, blonde, demure, though skinny. We passed in hall (my room was upstairs, hers down); we met in the common kitchenette. She asked to use my telephone and came up to my room and flirted on that pretext. Two nights after we met, we went out drinking and dancing, got drunk, and slept together.

She was French-Canadian, from Nashua, NH, where her father owned a department store; had been to junior college and was going to Harvard night school for an A.B., which her father scorned. Played the piano. Had been to Paris, where an artist had picked her up and gotten her pregnant. Had come back home for an $800 abortion from an elderly doctor, who later had slipped her a mickey finn and seduced her. Had a married man, a chemistry professor at Harvard, whom she had seduced. Worked for him as a typist late at night and made love in the coffee lounge. Had been doing this several times a week for over a year. Her parents, meanwhile, were verging on divorce, with her as their arbitrator. Father had been running with bad company from the golf club; father and mother had vicious fights; recently father had cursed mother and left, only to return to her after, her, Vicki's efforts. Also she had her best friend, Shelly, her ex-roommate, with whom she had had an affair a year or so before, and whom I'd like, and had to meet.

Vicki and I didn't last long—sex between us quickly grew apathetic, then mean—but before we lost interest, she did introduce me to Shelly, who had just moved into a new singles apartment building nearby. By contrast to Vicki, Shelly was all heart, energy, and gusto. Polish, also from N.H., platinum blonde, mesomorph, had had a year or two of college, age 24. By day a secretary at Polaroid, by night and weekends, the unabashed Doll Tearsheet, making the most of what she had. Smart, if not intelligent, with a prodigious memory, which she would show off at the mention of topics such as stalactites, Afganistan, asps, urban sanitation, mysticism, or current events. She was too plump and coarse for my taste, romantically, but otherwise we took to each other and shared some taste for escapades and characters.

Pete the Undertaker was one of her dates. Big spender, he took us all out in his Cadillac for drinks. He owned a chain of funeral homes and prided himself on practical jokes, such as pulling up in his hearse next to a housewife stopped at a light and going "Boo!" at her through a Dracula mask. He did have professional dignity, however, and when I asked him about Jessica Mitford's expose, *The American Way of Death,* said it was all lies and that he'd been on talk shows to offer the industry's response. "Listen," he confided, "it's no fun touching dead people, understand?"

Max, the Haitian Revolutionary, in exile from Papa Doc's police and dedicated to financing and supplying a rebel force, while clerking at IBM, was another friend and sometimes lover of Shelly's. He had also dated Vicki, and he would later become my friend and introduce me to the Harvard Square cafe pick-up scene.

But Shelly's real love was Paul Santos, a black insurance salesman, who was married with three children. Their affair had reached an impasse where they loved each other too much for half measures, yet Paul was unprepared to go public and leave his family, whom he also loved and had struggled and provided for and just recently had moved, as he put it, from the ghetto to a dream house in the suburbs. So he and Shelly were backing off from the affair, or trying to, still seeing each other, but openly seeing others too.

When Paul and I met at Shelly's, Paul sized me up, partly thanks to Shelly's introduction, as WASP, single, son and heir of a candy factory owner in Philadelphia, aspiring writer and graduate student, and to my credit as neither tight-assed nor a snob. He himself was light-skinned (part Portugese, from Chelsea), age 32, big-boned, round-faced with horn-rimmed glasses, and heavy-set, taller than I. He was playing chess with Shelly, presumably to show that he was a thinking man, with a new B.B. King record he'd brought playing in the background.

The chessmen were black and white, like life, he said. Though he was conventionally groomed and dressed, cravat, slacks, and new loafers, rather than say, Afro haircut, mojo beads and dashiki, he had Black Power slogans at the ready. Reparations were owed. If you weren't part of the solution, you were part of the problem. Black was beautiful. It was all good, let it all hang out. Got to get it together. Say what you mean or mean what you say or don't say it at all. Get with the program. Gotta have soul. As we discussed sports stars and jazz and rhythm-and-blues musicians, I understood "soul" to be a spiritual quality involving, first, the capacity and nerve to love life; second, wisdom about suffering and loneliness, and the need for human compassion and solidarity; and third, a oneness of the spirit with the body, and the body's needs and mortality. Chuck Berry, Otis Redding, Nina Simone and Janis Joplin had "soul," for instance, where Elvis or the Beattles did not. Shelly had it, where Vicki had not; and later Paul would flatter me: "You've got soul. Henry's a soul brother."

"You know my main men; know who I dig?" Paul announced. "Jack Kennedy and Martin Luther King. Kennedy was honest except he went for power at the end, and King because he said we got to live with the white brother, we got to live in the system. I'm a militant, don't misunderstand, but I work within the system."

From the start, Paul quizzed me about "broads"; confidentially, man to man, what about all those fine-looking women I knew, and how about turning him on to a few? When I answered vaguely about my not having much luck, just teasers and heart-breakers, he said these sounded like some sick women and he was going to have to show me some real women for a change. "Sounds like we could help each other out, Henry."

We became cruising and partying buddies, setting out at first with Shelly and her roommates, or sometimes with Max and others along to O'Dee's, a soul music club in Cambridge, or similar places, where Paul would pick up the tab. He drove a four-door, red GTO, which seated eight. Next, he started calling me at all hours: "Hey, Henry, what's happening?" Did I know any broads to party with? More often than not, I'd be studying, correcting papers or working on my novel or my thesis, but he would lure me out. We'd meet at one of the Cambridge cafes, or the Boston pick-up scene, new singles clubs like the Point After. As an odd couple, we combined black and white, fat and thin, flashily dressed big spender and economizing hippy, businessman and student, his ice-breaking, my apologetic sensitivity. Opener usually led to something like, "So how did two guys like you meet?" I don't recall our ever getting past the phone number phase with stangers; usually we'd end up, the two of us alone, drinking back at my Oxford Street apartment (into which I had recently moved from my rented room). He would lecture me. "Lookit, Henry, you got the crib, you got wheels, you're a good looking cat; you got to loosen up is all."

From, in living memory, being a lynching offense, interracial dating was just becoming fashionable, at least in Cambridge, combining the glamor of social guilt, protest, and experimentation with the lure of sexual adventure. The dynamics were charged. Though some people were romantically in earnest, many were reverse racists, on both sides, attracted more for the sake of the race than the person. For many black men, as for Eldridge Cleaver, whose *Soul On Ice* was just being published, white women (especially well-educated, middle-class white women) were viewed as the prized possessions of white males; to be openly preferred by such women, as men, as intelligent, competitive adults, was to defeat the "castrating" myths of the past. More than the so-called last frontier of sex; more than drug-induced new states of consciousness; miscegenation was the greatest unknown. For many white women, the attraction involved social idealism; some moral obligation to prove equality of race and to make a social statement. Other white women felt overtly freed from questions of marriage or social identity—still considering as axiomatic that interracial marriage and mixed race children were out of the question. Many white women also shared my own attraction to a familiar, yet different culture that corrected what they felt to be inhibiting and deficient in their own backgrounds. Officially, black women condemned the fashion of interracial romance as one of self-hatred and racial desertion, though I never found that attitude among the black women that I knew.

I must admit that at the time I was looking for white women who were bold and sexy enough to seek interracial sex—as if, as Paul had promised, they would be an antidote to the hungup intellectuals I usually dated, and I may also have harbored some fantasy of attracting them to my hip whiteness. I enjoyed many black women as cohorts and friends, but I myself was not looking for interracial sex.

Starting with secretaries at his insurance company, expanding through networks with downtown cronies and dating bars, as well as maintaining regular contacts in the black community, Paul knew—or set out insatiably to know—women from all over working Boston.

Somehow he had met a triad of roommates in Cambridge, with whom he fantasized staging an "orgee." Clara was the fine, tall black woman who interested him; Brenda, also black, he was fixing up with his cousin Hector; and Beth, who was white and a high school French teacher (he promised) would go for me. So first, the girls were having a party in their Linnean Street basement apartment. We all chipped in for fondu and liebfraumilch (exotica to me).

In the spirit of hearty, ribald fun, with Paul's social cheerleading seconded by Clara's, we did all get along, gathered cross-legged on the floor around the fondu pot, lancing cauflower, cubes of ham, tomatoes, and slices of garlic bread with fondu sticks, then dipping our sticks into the cauldron of white wine and swiss cheese, stuffing ourselves, drinking, dancing, and keeping up a loud, joking banter throughout, like a jam session.

Clara was a good match for Paul, bright, assertive, and sexually sly; Brenda, who was stocky and pigeon-breasted, got into an intense political discussion with Hector. Hector was thinner and handsomer than Paul; had been draft-dodging for two futile years, tried suicide, and was now a miltant, working as a supervisor of a Roxbury APAC. Clara and Brenda were friends from Columbus, Ohio; Brenda and Beth had met at the high school where Brenda was staff assistant and Beth a teacher. Beth was droll, tall, big-assed, a worldly single from a big family in Mattapan, who was comfortable with herself, had her degree from University of Massachusetts, Boston, had her job, and liked, as she put it, to let down her hair.

We started dancing. I'd come to pride myself on my dancing as Mr. Get Down and Dirty, Mr. Life, despite my loneliness and other pressures. Dance was in free-wheeling transition, so nobody really knew what was the latest, or what moves were genuine. I had evolved some crazy motion of my own, a hybrid, whereby I swiveled my hips round and round, and then snapped my fingers and did side steps from there, improvising; and pretty much, it sold. Some of my party-mates, in this case Clara and Brenda, would try to imitate and get it right: "Oh, teach me that! Hey, look at this!"

Following on that party, Beth and I dated alone, dinner at my apartment; we danced to Chuck Berry and to Janis Joplin, had lots of drinks, started undressing as we slow-danced, and then fell into bed. On separate, private dates, Paul and Clara had been getting it on, as had, presumably Hector and Brenda, or maybe not. Paul called me, then, wanting details, chuckle, chuckle. Said Beth had told Clara that I knew how to please a woman. Went on to propose a complicated trip, which he would pay for. He had a big insurance prospect to meet, a family friend of Clara's, back in Columbus, and Brenda wanted to fly home to pick up her car; so why not all of us go for a partying weekend? We'd fly out, stay overnight at Brenda's, drive back in her car. Don't worry about money. We'll have us that or-gee.

Though I was already tiring of Beth and had to teach Monday morning, and though Beth and I would be the only white people, I trusted Paul and went. Our jet climbed steeply from Boston—Paul loud, drinking and running his mouth at the stewardesses—then tilted down, descending, a two hour trip.

Our objective as Plain City, a settlement of ranch-style homes twenty miles outside Columbus. Clara's friend and Paul's prospective client, Charles Denton, met us at the airport, and drove us in his new Lincoln to Plain City, and to Brenda's where we were staying; later we would visit his home a street over for dinner. "We're just plain folks," he kept explaining. In his mid-thirties, he had fine-boned features, oriental or Indian, and smooth brown skin; he wore a black mustache and his hair was meticulously groomed; his long hands gestured languidly. He wore a white turtle-neck and dark silk suit.

We were welcomed as a party with high courtesy and down home warmth. "Clara's my girl," Charles told Paul. "You be good to her, hear? Rachel's my wife, but Clara's my girl." His home resembed my own family's in Villanova, outside Philadelphia.

After dinner, Charles, Beth and I sat around the kitchen table, smoking and drinking Black Bull, a 150-proof scotch; Charles's Uncle Bill had joined us, a tall, gaunt man with a lined face, white hair, and a mouth with a few scattered teeth. Uncle Bill was shaking his head and saying, "I just don't understand, I just want to sit and listen...I'm seventy-two years old..."

"You served your purpose," Charles told him, "now I'm serving mine." And turned to Beth and me. (Later I watched the old man, smiling toothily, reach out a gnarled hand to brush some spot of dirt off the shoulder of Charles's jacket.)

"Let me tell you something happened today," Charles continued, speaking to Beth and me. "These people called, these poor white trash. Guy works for me, wants to see me, a personal matter. You dig that?" His eyes held mine. "Okay, I said, come on by this afternoon. So guy drives out with his wife. They're all dressed up. Poor white trash. They see my house—they can't get over it, see?" He looked at Beth. "This was good enough for a rich white man's house; they'd never set foot inside a place this nice. So I showed them around, put on some tapes, offered them a drink. They meet my wife, my kids. They're looking all around; they're embarrassed, won't take a drink. Guy needs a loan of thirty bucks; baby's sick, kid needs clothes, rent's due. Well, now, this is the kind of guy—you're digging me—who's going to call me dirty nigger the minute he walks out. Well, I give a check says fifty dollars, not thirty. And you know what he says? He says, 'Mr. Denton, I want you to know I worked for a lotta different men in my time but you're the best boss I ever had." He waited for the meaning to register. "I told Paul tonight and Paul says, 'Whatta give that trash anything for? They'd kick you out on your nigger ass, they got a chance. You'll never see that fifty bucks again.' But I don't care if I don't see it again. See, that's what Paul can't understand. I'll get something out of it. One of these nights, some weekend, I'll be broken down and need a pull out, or I'll need a man, and I know now that man'll do me a favor." He winked and nodded slyly.

Later, when we were all drunker, he told us that he had come from a poverty background, a mining town in South Carolina called "Town Number Seven." Had used to run around on the streets in Columbus, and had only straightened out a couple years ago. His wife, Rachel, had straightened him out. "I used to work for the Man, you dig? There's this white cleaning outfit. They fire me. But we got a contract says they got to pay me a year's salary first; and I can't work, see, or set up any competition while they do. So I just sat around for a year. Then I set up a business, just a little business, actually, six hundred a month, and I was down there on my hands and knees scrubbing. They bought me out three months ago for $5000. I set up again with my brothers and now we're grossing eight thousand, man! In three months! We used to clean little offices. You get one account, do a good job, word goes out, you get two, three, four places, just me and my brothers, mainly. Now we've got three cleaning crews and we're doing all corporations and expanding to Dayton....These older folks, see, don't dig this; they've been working all their lives, and now I have it and I'm only 32. But I'm an old man. I'm not a brother, I'm a father." He wanted to die his hair white around the edges, he said, to lend himself dignity and austerity; he looked too young for his responsibilities.

I saw him as someone waking into a dream, uncertain of his limits, and as baffled by his actions as those around him were. He was the "new man," a function of the times, ambition, industry (as Horatio Alger might put it), and luck. Partly, I felt, he was dramatizing himself for Beth's benefit, and coming on to her; partly he was admiring himself in Uncle Bill's wonder; but in large part, too, he was performing for my white male approval and esteem.

We drove the grueling 700 miles back to Boston next day, and wearied by the chatter and hilarity of six friends in the car, I pretended to sleep, needing to be alone. Yes, Charles, I thought, I dig; we're all petitioners. All begging favors, even as we give.

Paul himself had achieved some affluence—he was in fact the "success" in his clan—starting with a degree from Boston University, which had been supported by his parents' lifetime of working at menial jobs. His mother had been a domestic, his father a laborer; he gave them money now. Affirmative Action under Kennedy had helped him find his place as an insurance agent for New England Life, and as other government programs, such as OEO and Model Cities, encouraged black capitalism, he found his insurance clients among the new flow of blacks into the business-owning and managerial classes, many of whom were previously uninsured and most of whom, like Charles, were readier to trust a "brother" than a white salesman. He sought clients on the grapevine and also was assigned targets by the company as their racial specialist. His roistering social life was also his business life, in that sense, a way of keeping clients happy and of cultivating prospects.

He'd been a fat teenager, homely and unpopular; had had to struggle to make friends. Had gotten his first girl friend pregnant and had had to get married too young to ever fool around. But now the lid was off. "I want bucks, booze, and broads," he would tell me jokingly, seriously, "though not necessarily in that order."

Within several months, Paul and I had become real friends, where I had had no close male friends since college. "If you were a broad, Henry," he said, "I'd be in love you, but I ain't." He went on to dramatize himself to my interest and appreciation, confiding in me as a full confederate. I did serve, in fact, as a credible alibi for him with his wife. Once or twice he asked me to answer, if she called me, that, yes, he had been out drinking with me on such and such a night. After one party at my apartment, he stayed over night, GTO in the driveway, and begged me to come home with him next morning as his cover. He'd tell his wife that he'd had a flat tire, and that he hadn't been able to fix it until morning.

Not wanting to get involved in this, I reluctantly gave in to his pleading, as a friend, and followed him in my car out the turnpike to Ashland, and through local streets, past open spaces, a driving range, older houses, into a new tract with streets of its own, to his big new house, a two-story Georgian with attic dormer windows, two car garage, flagstone path in front.

His wife, Peggy, opened the door, imminent with outrage, then saw me. She was attractive in a matronly way, light-skinned, careworn. Paul brusquely introduced us. And she restrained whatever fury she had ready, and struggled to put on her public best behavior and manners for my sake. Paul showed me in, invoking his pride and hers, their pride together in seeing themselves through my eyes. His kids—a girl 11, boys 9 and 6—hung back with a queer, nervous fear.

"We moved in last October," he told me, "isn't that right, Peggy?" Five rooms upstairs, study, boys' (Paul and Earl), bath, master bedroom, girl's (Nicole). Stairs. Raised living room with picture window and stereo and railing. Then foyer, dining room. Kitchen ("Want a beer? How about a beer, Henry?"—as he foraged for himself in the fridge). Den, with leather couches and a heavy corner table with on oversized Kon-Tiki lamp. And stereo speakers and walnut telephone, glass doors to patio, off kitchen then, laundry and bath.

He insisted I stay for lunch, settle down for beers and socialize, as if I had all Sunday. Peggy disappeared. With the kids, he barked orders: clean up this and this, turn off that music, get out and turn the sprinklers on, wash the car. All of which struck me as a sad, neurotic bullying, mental and physical, fueled by his guilt. "I teach my kids Black Pride," he proudly told me.

I got improptu calls, 7pm, say: "Henry, my battery's dead, and I'm at Government Center, can you give me a boost?" And I would stop whatever I was doing, as I would for family, and drive in, hood to hood, revving my six-cylinder compact enough to start his eight-cylinder behemoth. He offered to loan me money if I needed any, which I never asked.

He told me another time that he'd just returned from a hard partying weekend in Montreal and was lying in bed with his wife, when the phone rang and it was his mother, who started in about the ugly situation his sister was in with his no-good bum of a brother-in-law (she had gotten pregnant with a coil in and they had rushed her to the hospital, but no one could find the husband, and she might have been dying) and then started on about some one other of her children who had been running around with some white whore named Shelly, who used to live in Cambridge and now lived in Arlington, and he asked: who is that? who can that be? And she said, well, I thought it was probably you. And he: No. Are you off you head? All of this with his Peggy, whom he insists knows nothing about it because if she did that would be all, beside him. And now he had the question, how did this get to his mother? Did somebody look up Santos in the directory and know he came from Chelsea? Or did somebody Hector knows run her mouth and the grapevine carries?

He had other near-disasters at home: scratches on his back; lipstick on his underwear; names mumbled in his sleep.

He was like a secret agent, always at risk, always raising the stakes of deception: perhaps, I theorized, to defy his ordinary life—as employee, as husband, as father, son, as citizen—and to prove and celebrate a self freer and larger than his settled life allowed; perhaps, also, in some odd way, to revitalize and reappreciate his ordinary life by turning its simplest gestures into heart-pounding, death-defying acts.

His reputation grew. He introduced me to other, older and more successful black businessmen friends, who were into partying at a safe distance from home, free spenders, and interested in meeting white girls. Among these cronies was a vice president of Gillette, who was a prominent Black Power speaker. Another was a local politician, who earnestly demanded: how could I be wasting my time reading Shakespeare, when there was a revolution going on? Later, another white man, Jeoffrey Hughes, would join the circle; he was a Public Relations Professional from England, divorced, and in his forties.

In his boistrous, eager way, Paul urged me to throw big parties, and before long I was serving as a broker for such men, with my Oxford Street apartment a safe house, and they were paying me for it in terms of booze and party costs. They enjoyed my poverty. Who was it called me up—a corporate somebody—quite seriously, and offered me money to follow his white wife and report back to him? He knew she was screwing a white guy and he couldn't follow himself without being spotted, but no one would recognize me. I said no thanks, it wasn't my kind of thing.

I started reading to better inform my imagination: Richard Wright, James Baldwin, Eldridge Cleaver, Ralph Ellison, Malcolm X. Meanwhile, Jeoffrey Hughes was trying to start a company called "Uniloyal, Inc.," to offer "consultant services specializing in interracial affairs," and wanted me to run a seminar in black literature for upper level white executives, men like my father, for which he would charge a hefty fee in various cities. The idea was to help raise the consciousness of such executives and to better their understanding of their black employees. I already had more than I could handle, thanks. And the concept of the company itself soon proved short lived.

Time passed, and life went on for me in other ways, with other friends, while Paul would drift off for periods, too. I picked up girls now and then in the cafes with Max. November, 1968, I passed my PhD orals. I began researching my dissertation. Instead of teaching freshman composition, I was now teaching fiction writing to Harvard upperclassmen and enjoying the challenge.

I met a woman in the Idler with Max. She was sexy, streetwise and had grown up in Cambridge and Belmont, graduated from B.U., worked in an office for Eastern Airlines. Had travelled a lot. We dated steadily all spring. I met her parents, who were old enough otherwise to be her grandparents. I met her Cambridge friends, single and married. She did not like Joel, but did take the cause of race seriously and had gone South on civil rights sit-ins. She had friends at William and Mary, near Williamsburg, and once my teaching ended in June, we drove off to visit them and to have a lovers' weekend in Williamsburg, stopping off first to visit my parents in Villanova on the way. I had never brought a girl home before. Dad performed at his most charming. Mom attempted heart to hearts. They would tell me later, long after she and I had broken up, that they had known she wasn't "right"; that, in fact, they had detected that she drank secretly and too much, since the Beefeaters in our kitchen cabinet had mysteriously gone empty. Soon after she and I returned to Cambridge, she left for a summer in Spain, off her airline employee benefits; we would miss each other and promised to write.

Meanwhile, Paul called. Charles was driving to Boston with his mistress, Carmen, and wanted to throw a party in his suite in the Sheraton. Paul was closing with him on a big policy. So we all, Paul, Clara, Brenda, Beth, Hector, Shelly, and Max gathered to welcome him. Charles looked older, having in fact frosted his hair with white. Carmen, dressed in silk tights, resembled Ruby Dee: "She still excites me after all this time," he said, "just by coming into the room."

That August, Edward Kennedy, partying after his own fashion, encountered Chappaquitic with Mary Jo Kopeckni, and went on television to assure Massachusetts voters of his innocence. There was the moon landing. The Manson murders. I thought I saw an elision from moral-psycho explorations in fiction to life. People fantasized, made metaphors, read them, took drugs, then did them. The Viet Nam war kept worsening.

After some silence, I received a letter from my airline

agent friend dated weeks before saying that she had had a car accident and been hospitalized. She was healing but missed me. During her absence, at some chance Cambridge party, I met another woman, and as if in imitation of Paul, I started leading a double sex life. When my friend came back, she found out and we were finished. I saw her in a local bar a few weeks later and she wouldn't talk to me.

❧ ❧ ❧

Ed Williams, one of the few black students in my class from Amherst College, had shown up at one of my parties and we'd kept in touch; he was an architect and had a big pad now on Huntington Avenue, where he was throwing an or-gree, according to Paul, and to which we were all invited. That night Paul was at the top of his form, raging and outraging to the point of collapse, smacking his lips and clutching at his crotch, gyrating, bouncing and bopping his weight around as he danced, first with this "broad," then that, like a kid on Christmas morning.

He convinced several of us to promise to meet him for his parents' moving day tomorrow. Tomorrow dawned and he called at ten and told me to meet him at the Chelsea ramp off the Mystic Bridge at noon. I was waiting there, hung over and bleary myself, wondering whether he would come, when a horn blared and down the ramp, blaring, came the GTO, with, as they sailed by: Paul, with a checkered hat on, cigar in his mouth, his malamute dog with its head out the back window, and his wife in front beside him and three kids crowded in back with the dog. I pulled out to follow; then followed down unfamiliar streets, when Santos blared again and there was an answering blare across the square from Hughes in his Dodge as he pulled into line. Up hills, down, then Paul stopped to pick up a man he introduced as his father on another corner, and we finally pulled up in front of a tenement apartment house, got out, said hello, and Paul led the way up three flights to his parents' apartment.

He was trying, impossibly, to pull his life together; to have his extremes meet, as if somehow essences could agree where social realities forbid. "Henry, my Mother." I have no clear memory other than that she was proud of Paul, hardy, gracious, and good humored. We had lunch, chops and jag (a Portugese pilaf kind of stuff). Lots of beer. We struggled with dressers, refrigerator, beds, boxes of dishes. Hector was helping. Lowering the packed up and bundled dressers and desks down over the back porch with a rope. The move was only three blocks away, but to a first floor, smaller and more to their needs with the children grown.

That same summer, Jeoffrey Hughes told me that Paul was on the edge of doom. Behavior that before could be forgiven as hilarious had become increasingly reckless and sordid. Word was out, according to Hughes, that Paul had been screwing the Ashland wives, out in Ashland, which meant that word was getting to Peggy and her friends. Peggy had seen an attorney. "He's lynching himself. They're going to run him out of town on a rail. He's also in financial straits. He hasn't sold any insurance for three months. He's in hard debt. Hector has been given his IOU's to collect on. They're wondering about his usefulness at New England Life." Hughes went on to say that when he tried to tell Paul any of this, that Paul demanded names, dates, places. And if anybody told Paul about Peggy and the attorney, that Paul would go home and beat her up.

I felt naive that I hadn't sensed more hysteria beneath

Paul's recent escapades. I had, in fact, met one of the Ashland wives, Lucy, whom Paul had brought one afternoon to my apartment and then to a nearby motel. On my 29th birthday, he then had surprised me by bringing the woman's husband with him to my party as his cruising crony. Then Paul called Lucy, the wife, to tell her that her husband would be late. I marvelled at the psychology of Paul's seducing both wife and husband at once. Then he told the husband about Clara's tits standing up, when he knew (and had told me) that Lucy's, the wife's, were fallen.

When Paul told me that he and Hughes were no longer talking, I decided, as Paul's friend, that I must trust him as he wished to be trusted. In all his womanizing, I had only seen good humor and consent, never anything bitter, cruel, or coercive. If he ever did harm, it would be out of clumsiness.

He stopped by towards midnight one night, after dinner with clients, and started going through his numbers, calling up girls, and running his mouth. He was talking to some girl he'd partied with from his office: "...never been to Detroit. Didja tell her bout Paul Santos? Whatta mean she too old for me? Is she lookin' good? Aw, shit, I'll take some of that. Aw, she dusn' mind black cat? Whatta you mean, probably not, what I ask...you mean you know I been tryin to tell you t'take care of Paul Santos an fix em up, and you didnt tell her that you had the swinginest motherlovin cat in town? Oh, why the hell didn ya?...Sharon, I aint never gonna talk to you again. You piss me off. You have consistently got me aggravated...got me wid some goddam hot pants, you promised to take me to the Bahamas, you didnt take me there...n'wait minute, you got my dick hard, bout talkin bout other doggone broads, and youre screwin all over me...you play around with me too much...don't tell me one time that yer gonna straighten me out and then all of a sudden decide you want it all for yourself, cause I told you I can take care of you and her too. Now I already told you you couldnt handle me all be yourself...well, you can't! It's got nothing to do with you as an individual, its got to do with there is no one chick that can just handle Paul Santos, that's all. And uh you know like it's no big thing, but that's where it's at. That's the way my temperament is....All right, just don't tell me when nobody comes in, you know like do what you want, call Jeoffrey Hughes, call you know what's his name, Darnell, little short white cat with blond hair, looks like a doggone rat...oh, well, I injected him in the conversation. Because I decided to. All right, right. Why don't you just go out with Peter Humphrey, or uh, Bob Russell, and Jeoffrey Hughes and your other folks and just forget Paul Santos. That's all!... Sharon, good night!" He hung up.

I'd been laughing and shaking my head at his performance, but then he turned and said: "Henry, who are you to talk? You don't let these bitches fool you either. You can be cold when need to be. So don't think you are so different from me. You tell them where it's at. You do it in a different way, but it's still the same thing."

Clara was attacked that Saturday night. She had gone out to get milk at 9:30 and on her way back had passed and eyed a bearded man who then turned and seized her and gave her a beating, then fled when she fought free. He had torn her breasts out of her dress and crushed them. He didn't go for her purse or have time or place to rape her, so he must have just had psychotic anger, and wanted to hurt whatever she represented. If she'd called to tell Paul first, looking for some comfort and assurance, he must have disappointed her; and as she told me now the flatness of her voice felt like an accusation. I failed as well. I was sorry, but from so many removes. I even thought, somehow too readily, I recognized her attacker's rage.

A few weeks later I went alone to see Janis Joplin in Harvard stadium, August 15, 1970. One of a crowd of 40,000, I sat at the fifty yard line and the speaker system was on the fritz. Janis came out in dungarees and a pullover, just another scrubby little girl, and she was impotent without amplification. All that crowd eager to marvel at her, and here she was nothing, nobody, only some chick doing her wild gyrations way off out there, in silence. The three-quarter moon, bright, high over the other side of the stadium passed lower and lower towards the rim of the endzone seats before the speakers crackled on and we could really hear, just in time for her last few songs.

That labor day I went out to Paul's with a woman I liked as a friend and a fellow writer, whom I'd met in a local writer's group. Paul was in a new domestic mood, everybody happy and relaxed, barbecue sizzling. He took me aside at some point for cigars and J&B on the rocks, and said: "You know, Henry, I used to think I envied you, single, Harvard and all, but then one day I realized that you were hurting for what I got, the marriage and kids and house and family and the job with decent bucks; and that helped me to wake up to being who I am, you know."

I conceded that, yes, I envied him, offering up the words I thought he needed to hear.

We pretty much stopped running around together after that, as my own serial relationships seemed to me more painful and nightmarish; I struggled to finish my thesis; and inside, I was looking for permanence. Paul was right about that much.

PROMISES TO KEEP

After graduating from Amherst College in 1963, I lived in Manhattan for the summer and worked at *Redbook*, of all places. At night, I pounded out Kafkaesque short stories, which I promptly sent to The New Yorker and were rejected. In the fall, I headed for Cambridge. I had been granted a Woodrow Wilson Fellowship to the Ph.D. program in English at Harvard.

I found a furnished room near Harvard Yard; the on-premises landlord, a man close to my age dressed in a white dashiki, liked my "spiritual vibes." Apparently he had chosen the other nineteen roomers by similar means. Each side of the double-entry building shared a half-kitchen, a pay phone, a foyer mail table, and two bathrooms, accommodations reminiscent of a co-ed fraternity house. The owner had recently converted to the teachings of a stateside maharishi. He spoke of Nirvana and the spiritual path.

I signed into courses in Nineteenth-Century American Literature, Seventeenth-Century English Prose, and Sidney and the Sonnet Tradition (where we read the entire Arcadia). During lunch each day I reread *Anna*

Karenina for relief, feeling that this was my best substitute for life, while the rigors of scholarship otherwise preoccupied me. Graduate students at Harvard had no contact with each other and were treated coldly. The pressure grew so depersonalizing that I felt I understood when a fellow graduate student committed suicide in Inman Square by throwing himself between the wheels of a tractor-trailer, bouncing off, then trying twice again.

In late October I drove back to Amherst to hear John F. Kennedy dedicate the newly completed Robert Frost Library—an appearance, it turned out, just weeks before his assassination. He arrived late, by helicopter, then swept into our indoor track and field area in the gymnasium, where perhaps fifteen hundred folding chairs held guests, including me, and mounted the stage. A leather rocking chair had been placed there to ease his back, and the presidential seal had been attached to the podium. He spoke of writing as a national resource. "The nation that disdains the mission of art," he said, "invites the fate of Robert Frost's hired man, who had nothing to look backward to with pride and nothing to look forward to with hope." In Amherst terms, he sounded like an English major.

Back in my second-floor room in Cambridge, I stole hours from reading and from writing papers for my literature classes in order to write stories that emerged as forced imitations of the Transcendalists. Finally, come spring, I was convinced that my only way to leave Harvard and to write without being drafted—at twenty-three, I was being closely monitored by my draft board—was to apply to the Writers' Workshop at Iowa. Accepted, I took a leave from Harvard and was granted continued deferment for graduate study at Iowa.

With the blessing of my doubtful parents, I drove to Iowa City, where I continued to live in furnished rooms—

this time in an attic, in a single-family house, with the owners a young couple living downstairs with a three-year-old and a wailing infant. Two other roomers shared the attic, both Taiwanese, as were three roomers in the basement, where we all shared a bathroom and a kitchen. When the roomers' phone rang, someone would call out, "Yang-a-wa!" One night, late, however, the phone turned out to be for me, Richard Yates calling.

I had read and admired Yates's 1961 novel, *Revolutionary Road,* at Amherst, been surprised at Iowa to recognize his name among the fiction workshop teachers, and had signed up for his section. Later, we had met to discuss my stories, and he had persuaded me to get on with new work. Now, having just gone over a story set in my family's candy factory, he was calling to congratulate me on this as "the real thing" and to find out more about me. This had to be a novel, he told me.

With his encouragement, for the next year I lost myself in creative fervor, completing eighty pages. I was living, dreaming, and waking fiction, while also teaching freshman rhetoric at seven a.m., and taking Advanced Latin and Medieval Literature to continue progress on my Harvard degree. I even stayed in Iowa that hot summer, and was dismayed to learn that Yates had taken a leave to write a film in Hollywood, and that come fall, when I had been given a research fellowship, thanks to him, I would switch to his replacement, Nelson Algren. Unlike Yates, Algren disdained my work, saw me as an Ivy League snob and advised me to drop out and join the Peace Corps. My progress on the novel stopped. I switched to Vance Bourjaily, but still couldn't write.

I became aware of the Vietnam War as an issue. Iowa students held draft card burnings. Drugs appeared as commonplace. Hairstyles went to no styles. The birth control pill was made widely available. My first year at

Iowa I had no real contact with anybody but Yates. The second, I sought out social life from the undergraduates, not from workshop writers, most of whom I viewed as pretenders.

Meanwhile my parents back on Philadelphia's Main Line had moved from the house where I had grown up to a new "retirement" house in nearby Villanova. If I couldn't write, if I were only wasting precious time—career time—up the river, then I'd better go back East. At least the scholarly work was something I knew I could do.

I was readmitted to Harvard for fall, wrote the Cambridge landlord and got his best room, and with my savings from Iowa (where the cost of living was half of what it was in the East), I bought a new, not a used, car at home that summer. Settling back in Cambridge, I worked with Reuben Brower, a critic whose prose about literature was as clear as Hemingway's about life, and who had taught at Amherst. I felt challenged and impassioned again.

Having reached my twenty-sixth birthday, I could still be drafted, but the possibility was remote.

I was more a baffled witness to the public events of these years than an active participant. Intellectually, I was progressing slowly on my candy factory novel. I taught my first fiction writing class to Harvard upperclassmen in fall 1968. 1 was reading books about books to prepare for my orals, which I passed in November 1968, and then for two more years, while also teaching, I was researching and writing my dissertation on *Romeo and Juliet.*

The standout student in my fiction writing class was Kip Crosby, a twenty-two-year-old Harvard senior, who also became my friend and my self-appointed guide to a Cambridge underground, including folk rebels, druggies, nymphets, bikers, and hippie communeers, all of whom he saw as fallen geniuses.

He was crippled from birth by cerebral palsy, and would say of his girlfriend, Hilary, who was from a wealthy Jewish family on Long Island, "She thinks she is a freak; I really am one."

I had a poet friend, Bruce Bennett, whom I met first year at Harvard, and who had been away from Cambridge since, having finished his degree and then gotten a job at Oberlin College, where he shared in founding a poetry magazine, *Field.* Now, from the summer of 1969, he'd quit teaching and moved back to Cambridge, to concentrate on his poetry. He organized a writers group, which met in members' apartments; I was invited, and later I invited Crosby, and Crosby, in turn a woman from Madrid, my age or older, Leonore Aparicio Hushfar. Leonore had befriended Kip's girl, Hilary, thought her remarkable, and was aspiring to lead a literary salon herself; she also wanted to write poetry, and claimed to have been a disciple of Jorge Luis Borges during his residency at Harvard and to have read Robert Frost out loud to him. She, too, joined Bruce's group, and later she had parties.

My student/folk revolution/commune circle with the Harvard grad student and local writer circles. I saw this as a wayfaring from knowing no one to having choices.

Kip and Hilary passed on Hilary's Central Square apartment to me, while the two of them moved into a commune together. A woman I met at a Harvard party and dated led me to Peter O'Malley and the Plough and Stars pub, which had been recently rehabbed from a seamy taproom, where postal workers would drink, to a stylish recreation of an Irish literary pub, or to something like Dylan Thomas's White Horse Bar in New York. The Plough was on a corner just down the block from me. O'Malley, a tall, black-haired, hearty Irishman from Dublin, was the bartender. The woman and he had dated, and now he was planning to sail a trimaran to Rio de Janeiro, and she was tempted to join in, along with her four-year-old son. In addition to sailing, O'Malley's passion was music, in which he was taking a degree, and he would play the classical music station in the pub and give a free pint to anybody who could name that tune. He seemed to share my curiosity about people and my pleasure in commotion as forms of relief from serious, creative ambitions underneath.

Teaching had started for me again, meanwhile, and my thesis work had grown difficult. The woman and I soon stopped dating.

I was smitten, pretty much at first sight, by Connie Sherbill, whom I met in Leonore's apartment in the fall of 1970. Leonore had been taking a class at BU with Kip's girl, Hilary, and had also befriended an even younger BU student, who was Connie's roommate in a Brookline apartment.

Kip, Hilary, and I were at Leonore's for brunch.

Leonore hung crisscrossed chains on the window in place of curtains, had painted a slashing black and silver diagonal across the walls, had a tapestry hanging, and floors bare except for straw mats; also she had an expensive stereo system, exotic cappuccino to serve us, and a piano in one corner. At the time, a rock band was playing in Harvard Square, on the common nearby, its noise echoing in the street so loudly that we had to shout to understand each other.

The doorbell rang, then a knock at the door, Leonore went to answer, gave some excited greeting, and in came a short, plump girl, whom Hilary knew, hello, hello, and this other really beautiful girl, Connie. They had come over for the rock concert and then decided to drop by.

They liked that kind of music, of course! Didn't I? Connie was shy, but attentive and witty. Neither girl said much. She wore tight jeans and boots, and a vest; she was fresh and young, with full breasts, nice hips. shoulder-length brown hair, and eyes that sloped down, suggesting melancholy. I didn't ask her out, but I was driving back to my Central Square apartment and offered the plump girl and her a lift, dropping them off on the Cambridge side of the BU Bridge—stalwart, self-reliant, no-nonsense girls, I thought. I did ask Leonore about Connie later, suggesting interest. But I was involved with another girl, whom I found glamorous, and whom I'd met in one of Cambridge's continental cafes.

❧ ❧ ❧

Then Leonore had a party, supposedly a birthday party for herself; lots of new people, lots to drink, dancing. And Connie Sherbill was there because Leonore had remembered that I liked her before. Connie and I started dancing. A boy her age was trying to interest her, but I kept dancing with her, and when we sat down, I put my hand on a bare part of her back, and she didn't flinch. She was flushed and into the party. And in the salacious spirit of the night, I said: "How about going to another party in town? One special guy, Max, I want you to meet, is supposed to meet me there. How about it?" She said sure.

So feeling physical—did I kiss her in the car?—we found our way in town. When we got to the party it had wound down; people were stoned and dancing, but Max had been there and left, and I knew no one else. So we danced a while—I was trying to impress her with the dangerous, streetwise world I inhabited—and then I asked her back to my place, and kissing me now, flushed and excited in the car, she said yes.

Perhaps on our third, or fourth date, at my apartment, Connie got a phone call from her sister in Waltham that their father had just died.

Nearly every girl I had been serious about, from my first love in high school on, had lost her father; I seemed to respond to that, and they seemed to respond to my responding. Certainly I had the conviction that family tragedy made people more real.

Now I felt Connie's loss and wasn't afraid of it. With other women, people I really didn't love, anything this serious would be something to avoid. I also liked the sense of family in Connie's Jewishness, that family for her was at the heart of what mattered, which, in different ways, was my parents' creed, too.

Now, here, unexpectedly, after only two or three dates, I was facing her family grief and driving her out Mt. Auburn towards Waltham, where I had never been, out a winding, complicated main street I had never followed before, counting, and wincing as I counted, one funeral home after another, some seventeen in all (since then, I've realized that these were ethnic neighborhoods, Irish, Italian, Armenian, each with their own burial traditions, parishes, churches). Following her tearful directions, we found Brandeis, and across the street, the modern apartment complex where her older sister, Lonne, and brother-in-law, Larry, lived with their new baby. Connie ran sobbing into her sister's arms. Connie's date, a stranger to them, I was greeted with embarrassed politeness.

Next evening I went back with her, as the whole family gathered to sit shiva. Her mother, Hazel, and youngest brother, Ray, had flown up from Miami; her oldest brother, Danny, a rabbinical student, had come from New York. Her sister's in-laws, Mr. and Mrs.

Weinstein, arrived from Newton, along with their grown children. We went outside later, at Danny's urging, to stand in the chill fall night and view the northern lights, which dimly shimmered, thanks to a trick in the atmosphere.

❧❧ ❧❧ ❧❧

Connie had been born and raised in Miami. Her parents had been divorced only a year before, she said, "after twenty-four years and many attempts to patch things up." Her father, Joe, had been a truck farmer at one point, growing vegetables. Another time, which had involved their living in Panama, he had dealt in used cars. "He intimidated us," she told me, "but loved us dearly." They had had money at some point, but then had lost it. Generally, I gathered that he'd been luckless and intent on get-rich-quick deals. After the divorce, he had been alone, drinking, and financially destitute. Given that Connie loved him and was his favorite, she would torment herself now for not being there for him at the end. Deep in her own mind, he had needed her, and she had refused to see him when she could have; and she was to blame for deserting him and for his dying alone in a hotel room.

Hazel had had to rally first as a single parent after the divorce, and now as a widow. Having worked for her husband and having had to juggle an unpredictable income for years, she now made her living as a certified public accountant, while harboring passions for art, music, writing, and literature. She had put Lonne through college and seen her married to Larry in Boston. She had seen Danny, who had been a state debating champion in high school, through BU. Then Connie; then Ray still to follow. Connie's education had been financed partly by a student loan, which Connie would be paying off for years to come.

Connie, I felt, knew life in her guts. She believed in my ambition to write, and was ready to share in sacrificing for that ambition. She had majored in art history at BU, and her own ambition was to develop as a visual artist, and to teach young children.

By January 1971, she had moved in with me, and I would from our first sleeping together date no one else. I need to credit now, as I did not then, the effort for her I must have posed, given my age, background, and the momentum of my life. The space we shared was mine: my furniture, my address, my phone, my record player, my records, my décor, my habits; my desk and typewriter dominating the living room, where as I worked, she would study in the bedroom. My father might call, one of his random maintenance calls, and Connie would answer, and we'd say that she was over visiting, or over for dinner. We were always lying for appearances to the official world, which included Mom and Dad, and the landlord, at least.

By then my Shakespeare thesis had been accepted, and I would have my Ph.D., officially, come June; meanwhile I still taught fiction writing and freshman composition at Harvard and worked on the novel. Having spent a total of eight years rather than the usual four completing my degree, instead of having my pick of assistant professor jobs from a bulging placement file in the English department, I found the file nearly empty. My application letters for the few jobs that seemed appropriate failed to generate an interview. Even my most influential professors had no advice or leads. An oversupply of baby-boomers receiving Ph.D.'s and declining undergraduate enrollments had combined to bring on the unforeseen: an academic depression in the

Humanities, which would last, in effect, for the next ten years.

Kip and Hilary were married that Memorial Day.

When I turned thirty in June, I commented in my notebook: "I can't get a job. I can't have the things that normal people my age enjoy. I can't afford a family. When I was twenty-five, that was clearly a matter of choice. I was trying to be an artist, and I could always give up that ambition and still succeed by worldly standards. But here I am skilled, educated, and living alone on $4,000 where any stiff can make $10,000."

Connie graduated from BU and began working at a Head Start classroom in the basement of an Allston-Brighton church. Her BU roommates were breaking up. She took a room in Cambridge for appearances, but hardly ever slept there. Then in August, Mom and Dad visited Cambridge, and Dad assured me gruffly: "Don't worry about jobs. Persevere. You'll make it." For this visit, incidentally, Connie had had to hide her things and move back to her room, where we'd pick her up to take her for dinner or an outing, then drop her back off.

❧ ❧ ❧

The bar down the street from my apartment, the Plough, had put a sign in the window in the spring of 1970 asking for poems and stories for a broadsheet, and I had left a chapter from my novel there, shortly after I'd met the bartender, Peter O'Malley (whose sailing expedition to Rio had fallen through). As I stopped back months later, early in 1971, O'Malley told me that he liked the chapter and wanted to use it for the broadsheet, but the actual printing of the broadsheet had been stalled, because once they'd seen how much good work they'd gotten, they'd wondered whether they shouldn't be starting a magazine.

Would I be interested in working on something like that? he asked. I answered sure, having edited the *Amherst Literary Magazine* for three years; we shook on it, and arranged to meet in the pub later with the owner, some poets, and other literary "blokes" to talk about it more.

Through the spring, in the midst of everything else, we met at the Plough, in my apartment, or in O'Malley's apartment on Green Street. The founding group included my own friends, Bruce Bennett and Kip Crosby, myself, O'Malley, and O'Malley's friends or regulars from the Plough, Aram Saroyan (son of William, who claimed that his father had already done everything worth doing with fiction), George Kimball (a Hunter Thompson fan, who had studied at Iowa, run unsuccessfully for Sheriff of Kansas City, lived in the Bowery, then come to Cambridge to write for Cambridge's underground weekly, the *Phoenix*), Bill Corbett (a poet with ties to the Temple Bar and Grolier bookstores and locally prominent writers who gathered around them, as similarly tribal writers gathered around City Lights in San Francisco or the 8th Street Bookstore in Manhattan), David Gullette (an actor and poet who taught at Simmons College), and Norman Klein (a poet who had also studied at Iowa, knew Andre Dubus, and taught at Simmons). We settled on the name *Ploughshares*. We agreed on having a different member of the editorial board serve as "coordinating editor" for each issue, with me being the first. As our streetwise entrepreneur—and partner of the six or so Irish-American investors who owned the bar—Peter would take care of the business matters, printing, the paying of bills, distribution, and advertising.

Some of us—not me, thank you—were dedicated subterraneans, cultural mutineers (as Ronald Sukenick would later write) who had friends, counterparts, and heroes in the Bowery, in the Village, and in Berkeley. O'Malley boasted that the Plough was a place to meet others "whose failures are more glamorous than your own." Our motives were mixed, but none, give or take some notion of O'Malley's concerning publicity for the bar, were materialistic. I saw us as primarily refugees from other places where writing had mattered: in my case, Amherst and the Iowa Workshop. I had kept alive my own sense of vocation, somewhat, despite the rigor of Ph.D. work, in Bruce's writing group and in my teaching, and for me editing and producing a literary magazine was a still wider exercise of that vocation. Another excerpt from my novel had been chosen for the issue, and this would be my first publication since college; I was eager to share my best work, especially among other writers. I also felt the need to network and to publish as part of searching for a teaching job—and this was the motive I emphasized in long-distance calls with Dad at the time (he was skeptical, and made me vow never to put money of my own into such a venture; fine, so long as *it doesn't cost you anything*).

Over the summer of 1971, Peter and I met with Joe Wilmott, a friend and former student of Bill Corbett's at Emerson College. After dropping out of Emerson, Wilmott had gone to work for a South Boston printer, and having been granted after-hours run of the shop, had joined with poet Thomas Lux in starting The Barn Dream Press, a small press devoted to poetry. Barn Dream (named for what cows might think at day's end), in turn, had been inspired by a professor at Emerson, Jim Randall, who had been Lux's mentor, and who was bringing out Lux's first collection of poems from his own well-established small press, Pym-Randall. Lux was a serious poet that Bruce Bennett had come to admire while co-founding and editing *Field* at Oberlin. O'Malley and I, in any case, concluded that Wilmott was sensitive to poetry, altruistic, and otherwise sympathetic to our publishing goals, and would work with us in trying to keep down costs. Part of our deal involved Wilmott's contracting the typesetting, but then using my volunteer labor in the production process: proofreading, pasting up phototype for camera-ready single pages, and, later, opaquing and stripping the negatives for offset plates. We used an old issue of *Transatlantic Review* for our first dummy, imitating its format and pasting proofs over actual pages in the issue. All of this, of course, appealed to my teenaged hobby of letterpress printing, and, as I commuted by subway to and from the print shop that humid summer, and worked whole days in the shop's airless and un-air-conditioned darkroom, the old romance of craft engaged me, as well as the chance to learn offset printing, which seemed to demand more knowledge of darkroom photography than of operating presses.

I threw myself into all of this, in the face of ignominy, my struggle with my novel, and joblessness; I thought of my effort as one of personal rehabilitation, a way to use and prove my worth, regardless of whether established "society" wanted and was willing to pay for me. Connie, meanwhile, trusted and admired my commitment and supported its supporting dreams, as well as the long-term rationale with which I tried to explain it to my father.

In September 1971, the first issue of *Ploughshares* appeared, one thousand copies costing $2,000, a bill that O'Malley somehow settled with Wilmott's boss. Other than giving away copies to family and friends, we hadn't considered publicizing or distributing the magazine yet, but we printed a cover price both in dollars and pounds, to allow for O'Malley taking copies to Ireland. Kimball drove to Manhattan with a box and left some on consignment at the 8th Street and Gotham Bookmart. O'Malley and I left five copies here, ten there, at the various bookstores around Harvard Square. We tried selling a stack in the bar. Corbett knew a friendly bookstore in San Francisco and got them to order. We had a publication party in the bar, where a public broadcaster friend of O'Malley's interviewed us and then aired the interview on WGBH radio. Later the same friend got us to appear on a community affairs TV show, *Catch 44.* Thanks to Kimball and the *Phoenix* editors who drank at the Plough a full-length review of the issue appeared in the *Phoenix;* the reviewer was the Emerson professor, Jim Randall, who quipped that "*Ploughshares* is as much a happening as a literary event," questioned the compromises of our editing by committee, regarded the fiction as competent but unoriginal, yet ended by confessing "to liking both the magazine and its promise."

From the first, *Ploughshares* lent me social identity as a writer. Through that first issue and the sample of my fiction in it—about which Dick Yates wrote me, "Perfect, don't change a word"—I was taken seriously by writers my age who had themselves managed to publish books and land teaching jobs, among them Andre Dubus, Carter Wilson, Geoffrey Clark, Sidney Goldfarb, John Bart Gerald, and Fanny Howe.

❧ ❧ ❧

For fall 1971, I managed to continue teaching a section of expository writing at Harvard; I also was hired to teach remedial composition as a part-timer at Simmons College. The following academic year, however, I was unemployed, though I did keep applying for jobs, and in spring 1972, had turned down one offer to teach composition at Roger Williams College, in Rhode Island, where another student of Dick Yates's, Geoffrey Clark, had found full-time work fresh out of Iowa; and another at Wichita State in Kansas. Both schools seemed academically dismal; neither seemed worth relocating and giving up the promise of Boston for. Out in the cold—no income, no health benefits—I continued my volunteer work on *Ploughshares* and worked on my book, while I lived off of savings and Connie's meager salary from her daycare job. *Ploughshares* and its mission became so consuming that after forcing myself to canvas Harvard Square typewriter shops, bookstores, restaurants, bars, and clothiers in search of advertising, I would walk past new cars like an anarchist, angry at the unnecessary and indifferent wealth everywhere around me. *Ploughshares* became my social focus, extending to my conviction that there should be some average bracket of material need for each citizen, no more, no less, my version of socialism.

I had gone into partnership with Peter O'Malley in publishing *Ploughshares,* offering as capital my time and brains. In some way, too, I saw O'Malley and myself as an odd couple, complementing each other's strengths. Where business was concerned, O'Malley was the icebreaker, the commotion-maker, the fast-talker; then I was to do the follow-up and make the blarney real, as it were. O'Malley supposedly knew the ways of the world; I knew writing, editing, and scholarship.

From the first, however, I was committed to the magazine and its cause for keeps. And that would mean, before long—in addition to editing, pasting up in the print shop, distributing to bookstores, and selling and designing ads—having to take over most of the so-called business and legal details as well.

We opened a bank account under the name of *Ploughshares,* with O'Malley and me co-signers on all checks. We discovered grants. Bill Corbett knew Russell Banks, editor of *Lillabulero,* who was serving on the board of the Coordinating Council of Literary Magazines in New York, which sub-granted funds from the National Endowment for the Arts. O'Malley put in an application, friends lobbied friends, and we came up with our first $2,000 grant, which paid for Kimball's issue, but then, surprise, we had to show proof that we had matched this amount or pay it all back. At this point, I put in $800 of savings (despite my promise to Dad), and together with a supposed list of donors from the bar and our meager revenues, O'Malley managed to raise the rest.

Next, Connie heard about the Massachusetts Council on the Arts in connection with some Head Start project and urged us to look into it; O'Malley asked around and played his Irish political card—the Plough partners knew some powers at the State House—and we went into Beacon Hill and met with a very supportive Irish-American administrator at the Council, applied for and got another $2,000. Suddenly, between annual CCLM and Massachusetts Council grants, *Ploughshares* seemed possible after all, though we were now required to incorporate as not-for-profit and to apply for tax-exempt status from the IRS. O'Malley and a lawyer friend finally did the state incorporation, copying passages from a law book for our bylaws, which O'Malley regarded mainly as paper; properly bold and authentic spirits went ahead and parked in no-parking zones or lived on barter-and-cash rather than taxable income: up the system. The idea was to make the legal gestures and then do pretty much what you liked. He continued to view the magazine as a partnership between we two "directors," only instead of owning stock, we would accrue salaries on our financial statements, towards some eventual sale. The pro-bono accountant who recommended this was also accountant to the bar. From this point on, however, the future of the magazine would depend on "getting civilized." I insisted on taking over the checkbook. I did the grant writing and reporting. I dealt with the accountant. I learned nonprofit law.

❧ ❧ ❧

In my singles life, before Connie, I had taken pride in making one small room an everywhere. In clothes, in food, in furniture, in cars, apartments, in everything but books, I lived proudly at the poverty line—proudly because this was my choice, it had its ideology, and because like a mendicant monk, my eyes were not fixed on worldly matters. But as life went on, and as that became a life that I was asking Connie to share, my confidence in two sources of my eventual rescue from genteel poverty, in tickets back, as it were, namely a full-time teaching job and family money, wore thin, if not out. And outside of "the system," I was learning, you lived one day at a time, trading on your youth and chance.

Throughout this time I was, or felt myself to be to Connie, what I dreamed myself to be: the writer about to be recognized; the spiritual and sexual seeker settled down; the schooled scholar, critic, teacher, and editor, also about to be recognized and given cultural stability with a livelihood and a good job; the provider, family man, and father of children yet unborn, which had been put off only briefly until my promise was achieved; the branch of good Wasp stock, socially entrenched and better off than her own family, hence an upward opportunity in assimilated America.

We didn't rush into marriage. We talked about love, but never marriage. We were always mutually elective, a balance of powers; neither of us was without choices.

Marriage was only necessary for children, and children were only possible with a Real Job and income, and a Real Job could only be had, seemingly, either by compromising my dreams and accepting an offer like Roger Williams's, or by finishing and publishing my book.

Together with dreams, however, for Connie, there was always the uncertainty. "Do you love me?" she would ask over and over, never satisfied with the answer; if you had to choose between your writing and me, would you choose me? Unfair question, I would answer. If she had to choose between having children and me, or between her religion and me, what would *she* choose? It was the same kind of unnecessary, extreme question that you couldn't answer until you were faced with it as a real choice and either did or did not. She must have lived with the double prospects of my success and failure, even as she got up at dawn every day and took the bus to her Head Start job, which was bringing in our only income for the time being. What if some publisher, as Dick Yates expected, on the basis of the half of my novel that was finished, believed in its prospect of being finished, and offered a contract? What if the book was published, as my students' books—Nick Gargarin's and Kip Crosby's— had been, as Andre Dubus's, as Bart Gerald's, as Fanny Howe's, as Russell Banks's? If the dreams were achieved, then what would the next dreams be? Would I still love her, would I ever commit myself to the part of me that craved the completion of children and family, or would I only give parts of myself, like a tribute or toll, that I could afford to give? Would I, once I had some public recognition, look again to glamorous, pleasure-seeking women, women who had no imagination or desire to live risks with or about me, but only to enjoy the apparent benefits?

On the other hand, what if the book was never

finished, what if even I had to admit its flaws? Or what if it kept taking years and years, and then when it was finished, it wasn't published? What if all the doubters and nay-sayers were right? (And who, she must also have asked herself, who was she to question, given the years alone of this man, the complexities and experiences untold, the years of graduate school and teaching? And yet she was offering her life, and questioning was her right.) What if, indeed, realism was dead and even Dick Yates had no audience? What if there was some streak of self-defeat in Dee, afraid of real success or adulthood? What if time or love ran out?

✻ ✻ ✻

George Kimball was supposed to have been coordinating editor of the second *Ploughshares* issue, which we only managed to publish after delays and mishaps in June 1972; in fact, after the initial editorial meetings, George had vanished—rumor had it he was being sought for questioning by the FBI or CIA—leaving it to me to finish editing in his persona.

If the rotating editorship was going to work, we needed outside help—Kip Crosby, having married Hilary, had published his novel, and started acting as if his career had moved beyond the likes of us. O'Malley and I asked Jim Randall, since he'd reviewed us, if he would edit the third issue. Agreed. I also applied to Randall for a job teaching writing at Emerson, but he turned me down, in favor of Fanny Howe, "who had books." We started having editorial meetings in Randall's Harvard Street apartment, out of which he and his wife, Joanne, operated the Pym-Randall Press. Corbett and Gullette continued from the earlier group, joined now by the Poet-in-Residence at Emerson, Paul Hannigan, and a friend and former student of Bruce's, Katha Pollitt. Randall remained skeptical about my allegiance to realist fiction and my Harvard background, and I often felt the outsider among his circle. He had guest-edited an issue of *Sumac* and his Pym-Randall list was impressive, including Kenneth Rexroth, Robert Kelly, Allen Grossman, Basil Bunting, and Ford Madox Ford ("our only dead poet, because he is a personal favorite and his poetry has been neglected," he wrote), and he appeared to have made numerous literary acquaintances and friends over his past twenty years in the area. Given his creative writing program at Emerson and his literary convictions and friendships, he was the unofficial pope of Cambridge literary life, excluding Harvard; he himself had graduated from BU. His literary court, other than his apartment, was the Toga Lounge across from Harvard Yard, and his way station was the Grolier Book Shop. He brought a new level of credibility and of contacts to the magazine.

We agreed that I would do an interview with Richard Yates for his issue. Geoffrey Clark, who had had a story in the Kimball issue, had invited Yates for a reading at Roger Williams College in April, at which time I drove down, and Clark and I questioned him together. I later transcribed the tape and patched together a draft, sent it to Yates in Wichita, where he was teaching; Yates rewrote, cut, and added; I then offered extra questions by mail as well as a draft of a concluding statement about neglect and fame that I thought he should make—in all of this I was inspired by a cover interview that James Alan McPherson had recently published in the *Atlantic* with Ralph Ellison. Randall was happy with the result.

About this same time, O'Malley asked me if I knew anything about Richard Wilbur, and I said sure, that together with Robert Lowell, I thought he was the best poet since Frost. Peter took that in, then explained that he'd been seeing Wilbur's daughter, Ellen, here in Cambridge, that she was a writer, and would I mind looking at some of her stories and poems sometime. Before long they were engaged. Connie and I were invited to meet Charlee and Richard Wilbur in Ellen's apartment in one of the Harvard houses, where we stayed up most of the night drinking, telling stories, and singing along to her brother's guitar. I was dazzled. O'Malley as a quantity seemed to challenge them much as he challenged me; Ellen, with all her natural elegance, heart, and intellect, had somehow set out to redeem and direct O'Malley's raw energy (his "daemonism," as I described it to Yates), and to help him foster his talent as a composer. As a gifted writer from a writer's family, she also believed in the magazine and added to Peter's commitment to it. They were married that summer, and Connie and I stopped by their big wedding in the Berkshires, then drove on down to Philadelphia to visit my parents, where Connie argued heatedly with my father about McGovern and ending the war, and we visited my grandmother in her nursing home, as well as my second oldest brother and his family in New Jersey, and went through all our family photographs.

Nixon was reelected. A cease-fire was called in Vietnam with the New Year. The early Watergate hearings began. By March 1973, the draft had ended and U.S. forces were leaving Vietnam. Spring, I worked with Thomas Lux in editing the fourth *Ploughshares*. Also my writing was getting attention.

Finally, Randall hired me as Emerson's Prose-Writer-in-Residence from July 1973 to 1974. The pay was $4,000 to teach two workshops, and at the time it seemed like a rescue and an affirmation. A job in the world lent force to my faith, not only to continue with *Ploughshares,* but to marry Connie.

ON MY RACISM

NOTES BY A WASP

That citizens of color must confront racism daily in America's traditionally white power culture is no news; nor is it news that white citizens, for the most part, being able to, are more likely to ignore and to evade both their own racism and that of so-called minorities which is directed towards them. By inclination, I find myself accepting the social evil of racial hatreds, accepting the ignorance on which they are based, and their psychological mechanisms (such as scapegoating), as inevitable, the way war is inevitable, or the way natural disasters are inevitable. So when an African-American man, a decent man minding his own business, is lanced with an American flag-and-flagpole by a white American man in the courtyard of Boston's City Hall. I deplore the fact and deplore the image in the newspaper and on TV—the two faces twisted, one in hate, the other in astonishment—but I also accept the racial hatred philosophically, allowing for it as the sorry way of the world. I needn't feel it personally, with personal anger, as if there were anything to do about it, for me or for anyone. I am neither the sick individual bearing that flag, nor the individual victim, selected as randomly, seemingly, as any victim of misfortune. In my acceptance, of course, I am refusing to confront racism. I am avoiding or ignoring the fact.

❧ ❧ ❧

I live in Watertown, Massachusetts, a suburb west of Boston where my neighbors are white, mostly blue-color, mostly Italian- and Irish-American, mostly Christian. Homes here, in a forty-year-old development of two bedroom capes, ran around $180,000 on today's market, so there is a certain respectability, and a taxpaying involvement in society. Moving into our house and yard five years ago, I was sensitive to the neighborhood's customs, the well-cut lawns, the gardens, the shrines, the Christmas lights. We have some Asian neighbors a street or two over; no black, though one black teen-ager from time-to-time on the park basketball court. I was shy of sticking out, of becoming any sort of target. I didn't want to appear bookish. I didn't want my wife Connie's Jewishness, the flicker of Shabbat candles on Friday nights, a Chanukah menorah in the window, or the absence of a Christmas tree, to advertise difference. I had conceded, perhaps too easily, that this was *their* world, their norms, their majority. I wanted to be taken for belonging, whether in truth or in heart I actually did.

❧ ❧ ❧

Am I a racist? Yes, as I am fallible in many ways I know and don't know and mean better than to be. But just as I am aware enough of envying, say, the rich and famous not to indulge or sanctify my envy, so I need to be aware of my thinking and feeling about race. I am not socially disadvantaged because of my own WASP appearance and culture. I need to remember that. I need to remember that my attitudes about equality and tolerance and mutual regard are in all ways necessarily privileged attitudes, expanding from an unembattled confidence in self, or at least in those aspects of self that a powerful and self-confident culture approves.

❧ ❧ ❧

My wife's Jewishness has been both an enriching and uneasy difference to me over our eighteen years together; at different times I have wished that she had her values and personality and unquestioned membership in my native *tribe*; and she has wished as often, all other things being equal, that I were Jewish. We saw our intercultural marriage as a challenge from the start, or told each other so; we knew that it would take work, some loss on each side, and we had proved to be positive partners over these years, while relatives and friends divorce around us, having found differences other than our obvious ones impossible to reconcile.

I both respect and question her efforts at religious observations in our family life with our twelve-year-old daughter, Ruth, and our four-year-old son, David. Friday candles. Chanukah as well as Christmas, Passover as well as Easter. Issues of circumcision for our son; bat mitzvah for our daughter. My wife speaks to me of the beauty to her of her religion, which she wants to pass to our children, and of her grief in having to mute that part of herself as part of her rapport in marriage with me, a grief I must allow. I react to what strikes me as Judaism's irrationality; and to the tribal presumption: Jews have suffered. Jews are the chosen people. Fail to observe your Jewishness and you are part of the problem; you abandon those who have suffered and been murdered for the sake of your identity. I respect all this with conscious effort. I enjoy her family, her widowed, independent mother, an older brother who is a Conservative rabbi, an older sister, a younger brother—all married to Jewish spouses, and all spiritual, serious people in ways I understand apart from formal religion, people who question and who value life, family, and society. And people, I should add, who have accepted, supported, and tolerated me and my difference over the years. Nonetheless, when I am on their terms, immersed in their tribal culture, for Connie's younger brother's wedding in Miami, say, I feel alien. I don't choose to be irreversibly different in a surrounding where I am a contradiction or a minority, self-effacing and politely on my best behavior.

I also dislike befriending and socializing with other people (as Connie has sometimes seemed to do) primarily because they are Jewish. On one occasion I felt threatened and jealous to hear that such-and-such knew their single Jewish lawyer friend, whom we'd met once or twice at their seders, to have a crush on Connie. And I feel troubled to have my daughter reciting Shabbat prayers in Hebrew, prayers I can't (or won't) learn or understand—as if now she's become one with a world that excludes me—and to have pressure from Connie's family to raise her as fully Jewish.

What I perceive as our fair balance of both cultures, Connie perceives as unfair since, she maintains, I have no serious religion of my own, and since the dominant Christian culture is everywhere around us, *on my side*, as it were. On the other hand, her family is much younger than mine, and more present in our children's lives. My mother died when my daughter was seven, time enough for a strong bond to grow between them and for lasting memories. But my two brothers and sister, ranging from six to eleven years older than me, are rooted in lives different in ages and stages from ours, and are unreach-ably distant in miles as well. Where Connie's family has had annual reunions and frequent visits, and where my daughter can relate to cousins near her age (all of whom visibly practice organized religion), my brothers and sister and I have had our reunions only at our father's—and then ten years later, at our mother's—funeral, we've rarely called, written, or visited, and their children are grown, scattered, and having children of their own. I do have a background and culture of my own, of course, one I feel exiled from and nostalgic about passing on. It is not a culture as simply stated as a religion or as religious tenets, and part of my problem is in trying to state it at all, to become more conscious of who I am, tribally.

In the process of these years, Connie and I have learned to trust and respect each other's different values and feelings. This two-way balance has taken *work*, but it has been for the sake of deeper needs, beliefs, and responsibilities we share.

❧ ❧ ❧

Most American writers and readers seem to avoid or ignore racial issues. Again, writers of color have always had to pay attention to the power culture; in their daily lives they must confront its members and its institutions, and they have had to imagine daily the inner lives of white and mostly Christian Americans, read, hear, and see their self-advertisements, their fictions, their films and TV shows. When a "minority" writer writes, there is also the challenge of double audience: she or he wishes to voice and dignify the experience of a separate culture, and hence writes to members of that culture; but his or her address is mostly to the white majority—the market necessary for profitable publishing. White writers who address race are rare, because, again, they have not felt the necessity—material or moral—to pay attention, and they presumably perceive no urgent interest in race in their white reading audience. William Faulkner, following on Melville and Twain, was an exception; likewise Katherine Anne Porter, Eudora Welty, Bernard Malamud. There is considerable risk in this, as the controversy surrounding William Styron's *The Confessions of Nat Turner* should recall. My own admission as a writer is that I don't feel I have the experience; I have not paid enough attention in my life to imagine the inner life of any person of color in America.

❧ ❧ ❧

My racism was involved in adopting our son, David, who is Korean. Other *isms* were mixed up in it. Biological chauvinism, for instance. I desperately wanted a second birth child; Connie wanted a child, period, and had no problem with adopting. But I could not accept my or our secondary infertility at first. Once I finally did, I did not want a child who looked like us. The idea, however we sought a child, and however much it matched our body types, eye color, and complexion, supposed a lifelong deception outside of the family, and neither of us welcomed that prospect. We had been through enough with the infertility ordeal and then with a survey of various donor options. We were told that white-to-white domestic adoptions were hopelessly expensive and involved delays of one or more years. Connie felt that she couldn't wait any longer, that already the age difference between our daughter and any sibling was at its maximum. We heard, at this point, of an excellent, nearby international adoption agency, and agreed on our preference to have a non-white child, a child whose adoptive status would never be a secret. This was sharing the problem in my mind, and also it deepened the commitment to our balance of cultures in the minds of both our families. We visited with a white couple who had adopted two black children, also with a local librarian who had adopted an infant from Brazil. Black children, American or otherwise, were no longer easily available to white couples, but at some point we did discuss the possibility, and I did not feel that *I could take on society to that extent, that this was a battle I could choose.*

My racism at that point phrased itself as a social fear. Later it was phrased as a cultural preference. Given the choice of international programs among 1) Indian, which we were told some couples preferred because Indians have Caucasian features, 2) Asian (Cambodian, Korean, Filipino), and 3) Central American (Salvadoran, Guatemalan), I favored the Korean program, with its system of orphanages that had been in place since the end of the Korean War. The health of babies was said to be excellent; also, education was highly valued in Korea and the fact that both Connie and I were teachers promised our acceptance. But mostly I told myself that I would study my child's culture with him or her, and that we would inevitably meet and befriend other parents and children from that culture, and perhaps one day visit there. I was attracted by Asian cultures because of my impressions of Eastern history, religion, and art, and because my sister's husband was half-Indonesian, half-Dutch. Also, one of my brothers had served a postwar Army tour in Korea, been moved by the plight of orphans there, and had taken hundreds of slides; a surgeon now in New Jersey, divorced, with three grown sons, he supported our choice.

My son David Jung Min Henry is now nearly five. He is a Jewish Christian Korean American. His face to me is as familiar, expressive, and unique as my own face. Nothing seems more natural.

⁂ ⁂ ⁂

In James Alan McPherson's story, "Gold Coast," the narrator says with characteristic irony: "I had forgotten that I was first of all a black and I had a very lovely girl who was not first of all a black...she believed with me in my potential and and liked partly because of it; and I was happy that she belonged to me and not to the race." In the course of the story their relationship is eroded by "social forces" that they can mock and withstand at first, but to which they ultimately succumb. Neither is worth that prolonged effort to the other. "We aged...there was nothing left to say."

⁂ ⁂ ⁂

I was mistaken once in the Seventies by rednecks cruising in Cambridge for a "hippie scum" because I wore striped bell-bottom trousers as a kind of personal joke. They pinned me to the wall of a corner bar with their car bumper and shouted obscenities at me. But it wasn't *me*. Mistaken identity is the expectation of groups stereotyped by the power culture.

⁂ ⁂ ⁂

I have grown over time to recognize and value racial or cultural differences as essential to individuals I value. I do not want my son to be white. His racial difference is inseparable from his personality, from the remarkable person he is.

I think of Sir Thomas More's criticism of social evils in 16th century Europe, *Utopia.* I think of his shrewd and realistic suggestions for how education and carefully designed social values might eliminate (today we would say sublimate) tyranny, greed, and violence. Hunting would be abolished as a rehearsal of war skills and blood lust; war heroes would not be celebrated, but in their stead, in all public spaces, philosophers would be the subjects of sculpture and cultural praise. Perhaps in regard to race we must be more utopian. Civilization is of necessity utopian in aspiration and direction without being sentimental or simplistic. Machiavelli was another Renaissance utopian, according to some recent historians. A culture, a society, cannot be structured without confronting—without an unflinching awareness and understanding of—its negative propensities.

We are in an adventure now, on the threshold of the 21st century, of aspiring to a world culture, a global "Good Society." Within American society by the year 2000, we expect citizens of color to increase to thirty percent of the population, and the day is coming soon when white citizens will no longer be a majority. Meanwhile, extremist white hate groups are forming networks. Racial incidents are occurring among students on college campuses. Citizens of color are speaking of an impending race war.

Thomas More found the social evils of his time to be rooted in self-destructive appetites and in institutions that seemed contrived to "activate human wickedness and anesthetize human decency." He was an "alienated intellectual, an intellectual who did not accept the validity of the assumptions, objectives, and rewards of the power system of the culture he lived in." He would, I imagine, applaud the ongoing analyses of the "power system" in our racially troubled times and advise us to continue to reform existing institutions and create new ones in a way that activates benevolence and stimulates decency. He would also advise us to teach according to our consciences, as unattached intellectuals. "True teaching needs free speaking, and never more than in a sick society." (All quotations from J.H. Hexter's *More's* Utopia: *The Biography of an Idea.*)

If there is hope for our civilization, perhaps it lies partly in the "true teaching" of honest, confrontational writing.

Hope also lies in the positive energies of difference, in new insights and perspectives on common problems, in contributions by different cultures to all aspects of our national culture, and in the personal growth, individualism, and self-esteem that come from recognizing and cherishing the worth of others.

AN INAPPROPRIATE MAN

He was Middle Eastern—Iraqi, Iranian, Lebanese, I guessed—forty years old, dressed in what looked like white pajama pants and shirt, black hair, perhaps 5' 8", 160 pounds. His complexion was dark, but not Indian dark. He wore sandals without socks. All day, from as early as 7 am, he walked and paced and roamed our neighborhood. We saw him as we drove, or biked, or went about our lives. He seemed to have no job. He was always *there*. On the neighborhood playground outside the kitchen window of our three-bedroom cape, which stood across from one corner. He smiled and watched the young children on the swings and their mothers. He was there in all seasons, though I recall him mainly from spring and summer and cannot imagine him in an overcoat, hat, or winter gear.

He lived in a three-bedroom cape, like the others, though it changed owners more frequently, some five or six times during our ten year stay here. This grid of cape houses from a thirty-year old development in West Watertown, and depending on the real estate market range from $300,000 to $600,000 in value. Many of the working class owners living here have had some connection to the once massive Raytheon complex a mile down the street, along the Charles River. Others have moved in, as we did, for starter houses, with jobs in high tech (the famed Route 128 computer-related companies are ten miles west) or in some sort of white collar work in Boston (ten miles east).

As we drove past his house—we knew it was his because we saw him exiting or entering there randomly—sometimes we saw women, one, two, perhaps three different women of indiscriminate age, wearing again, Iranian, Iraqi, or Arabian veils, heads wrapped in scarves, bodies covered in loosely draped foreign dresses. They did not walk the neighborhood and rarely if ever seemed to venture out. We saw no car, though they must have had one for shopping. We never saw him or them in the local supermarkets, liquor stores, cleaners, laundromat, post office, or library. There was no sign of children.

So the man walked. From early morning, weather permitting, to afternoon, to late at night. Pondering, it seemed, over our foreign environment.

But what was he doing here? The more conspicuous and public he became, the more we felt embarrassed by his oddity. He spoke to no one, and likely could not speak English. No one spoke to him.

My writer friend from Iowa City, James Alan McPherson, visited one summer and I pointed out the man to him. Jim peered out our kitchen window and asked, "Why don't you just go up to him and ask him who he is?" At least this was a writer's, if not a neighbor's obligation. (Jim, of course, was preoccupied with the idea of neighborhoods, writing about and creating his own locally in Iowa City, and globally and spiritually with friendships ranging from Japan to Baltimore, Boston, and his original neighborhood growing up in Atlanta, Georgia.)

My answer was shyness, or incuriosity, or prurience—I didn't want to pluck out the heart of the man's mystery. Jim and I joked and conjectured about him instead. Probably the man had been relocated by the government as some soft of CIA payoff for spying. He and his wives and/or daughters. Probably the man kept his women strictly cloistered from what he saw as a corrupt and corrupting world. He locked them in the house all day working on sewing machines or cutting and refining drugs or some other cottage industry. Even joking, Jim and I never imagined the man to be a novelist or a writer who was studying suburban America, Salman Rushdie incognito, perhaps.

Over time, I had a queasy feeling about the man as a possible child molester. The way he lingered at the playground. Somehow his walks conveyed predatory, leering lust. Not just a lurker, peering in lighted windows. Not just a time-passer.

On the corner across from us were Lawrence and Janet Kessinich and their two young children. Their first house. Lawrence had been an editor at Houghton Mifflin and had published Thomas Kinsella's *The Field of Dreams* and had had some hand in the movie deal that followed. But then had become disillusioned with publishing as a business and quit in order to go back to school and become a therapist. At the time, while I chaired Emerson's Writing, Literature, and Publishing Department, I hired him as an adjunct to teach graduate publishing and editing courses, which he did with distinction for several years. Jan taught piano, and briefly my wife Connie had been able to get her work at the nearby private elementary school, where Connie herself had established her career. They had invited us for dinner once. Connie and

Jan had tried walking together for exercise. But the friendship didn't work out and grew to keep a cordial distance.

Connie was visiting Jan one day, offering a joint yard sale off the Kessinich's front lawn and driveway. An all day enterprise, where neighbors and strangers stopped by to examine goods, bikes, stereos, chairs, skates, clothes, lamps (often bought at someone else's yard sale) and to haggle.

Connie came home that afternoon and said that the Inappropriate Man, who lived three doors down and across the street from the Kessiniches had approached her and Jan and that he had suddenly seized her, Connie —my wife—and kissed her on the mouth. At which point she and Jan both had said, as if to a child, firmly: "No. That is inappropriate. We don't do that here."

I wondered what my place as a husband was at the time. This had happened hours before. The man hadn't desisted and had tried again, but both Connie and Jan had been firm. Telling him, "Stop. No. The is not allowed!" And ignored him until he finally wandered away.

Jan had said she thought he was harmless, just confused. Probably in his country a woman with an unveiled face was considered to be a prostitute, inviting, and fair game. He was suffering from crossed cultural signals.

I had less generous opinions.

Should I go warn him? Threaten him? Act the offended husband to the disrespectful Don Juan? Should I call the police to warn him? Was he arrogant? Was he dangerous? Perhaps as a Middle Eastern Muslim, he recognized Connie as Jewish, which rendered his advances either as a bid for separate peace, or as contempt. In any case, I saw him as sinister, while the women dismissed him as harmless, ignorant, and confused.

I also had my daughter to protect.

The inappropriate man walked more and more often past our lightened windows, I thought. He tried to catch my eye. *How could I not accost him?* he seemed to be wondering. *What kind of a man was I?*

✻ ✻ ✻

Shortly afterwards, he vanished; his family vanished, poof, without a trace. The house was sold and vacant. We have no idea what brought him here, and no idea what caused him to move in; how, or where. My guess is that money ran out. But who knows? Maybe just the opposite.

The house has been sold three more times since. It is our neighborhood's quick turn over house.

WRITING FROM EXPERIENCE

I had a debate once with the novelist Margot Livesey about whether the death of a talented person was any worse than the death of anyone else. She maintained that it wasn't; and I maintained that it was, because we mourn both the death of the person and the death of the talent.

Some years ago there was a student death at Emerson College, which moved me, though indirectly. Sally Arkin* had been my advisee for three years and the fall before had taken my course in Shakespeare's tragedies and despite her uneven attendance she had earned an A. She always sat next to a slow witted boy named Walt, whom she helped to revise his papers, and to earn a B. In class, she was genuinely involved with the poetry and the questions of the plays. Her term paper on feminist approaches to Shakespeare was forthright, direct, and full of individual voice and intelligence. I left it with an A in my box, along with the comment that she should submit it for a Dean's Prize. End semester.

At the end of January, that same academic year, I got

---

* Names of all students have been changed.

a call from Elizabeth Searle, with whom I had some professional history. I had published one of Elizabeth's early stories when I was editing *Ploughshares*, and then had hired her to teach at Emerson, while I served as department Chair. My blurb appears on the back of her prize collection, *My Body to You,* to the effect that she "invests perversity with a strange innocence." In any case, time passed, and she taught well and was paid well. Then I was replaced as Chair and she was still kept on part-time into the new teaching year. She was calling me now because one of her students in senior seminar in fiction writing had just died of a drug overdose in the arms of his girl friend, another one of her students. The victim's name was Bruce, and the girl friend's was Sally. Sally had called her. She herself hadn't known whom to call at Emerson. They were all friends. Bruce was gifted. I asked, Sally, not Sally Arkin? Yes, Elizabeth said, did I know her? It shocked me that Sally Arkin, as a bright, clear-headed and clear-hearted person, should be into that heavy a drug scene. I told Elizabeth to call Emerson Security and to get the Dean of Student's number and to call him at home, and to tell Sally to call me if she wanted. I was concerned.

From Sunday to Tuesday morning, when I went in to teach, I gathered that there had been some rallying around the tragedy. Jonathan Aaron, Bruce's teacher in senior thesis, had been called by and met with Bruce's bereft parents on Sunday for brunch. The Dean of Students was issuing a memo college-wide. Robin Fast, our undergraduate coordinator, had talked with Sally, also a student in her class. John Skoyles, the new chair, had been notified but not called in to deal with the situation. Jonathan told me that there might be legal problems for Sally. Bruce had never taken drugs. This had been his first experience. They had been at Sally's mother's house, and Sally had had powdered heroin, which she had introduced to him as a risk and an adventure. He had been a very talented, handsome kid, according to Jonathan, who had also studied with Sam Cornish, Joe Hurka, our best; he was only months from graduation.

I taught my Shakespeare class on *Merchant of Venice*, wolfed lunch, and had just settled into my office when Sally herself appeared. Without a word, I gave her a hug of sympathy. What she wanted from me as her advisor was to tell her other teachers what had happened. And that she didn't want to take a leave of absence; that it is was important for her now to work and to finish the semester. I told her simply that she was someplace I had never been. She wept then with the full right to cry, a level person leveling. She had been living with and loving the boy, Bruce, she told me, whom she knew to be remarkable. Yes, they had been using heroin, not junkies, just experimenting, and she had turned him on. She had meant for them to celebrate his just having heard that his first story would be in the college literary magazine. And then she knew he was dying, overdosed. Called the ambulance. Knew he was dead, outside. And beyond feeling guilty, felt and was feeling the grief, the loss. She wanted to talk about him. She wanted to bury her face in his clothes. She and Bruce's friends were organizing a Memorial Service for that Friday, and she hoped I could come.

I made the effort to attend, driving in on my day off after teaching all day and night Thursday. Bruce Watkin's obituary had appeared in the *Globe;* there had been an article and editorial in the student newspaper, and memos had gone out to students and faculty. The memorial was held in the chapel of First and Second Church. It was crowded. Elizabeth and her husband were here, and Elizabeth's husband had arranged for and set up the sound equipment. The service was a celebration of the life, sober and relatively dry-eyed. There was a program. Bruce Watkins had been a campus personage. As a young man, he was writing about the edges of his place and time, phone sex, porn, eros, technology, cyber stuff, religion and the conflict between feminist manners and hormones. As Sally and other friends read from his stories, I was impressed by his charming, arch, Salingeresque mania. And in the heart of all this, I was also impressed by Sally Arkin's aplomb, like one of life's insiders. There was nothing corny in the service; nothing self-serving or vain. I told her that she ought to organize a chapbook of Bruce's stories with an introduction. She was at the threshold of adult life in a position something like Tess Gallagher's in mourning Ray Carver. She turned during the service and took my hand. "Wasn't he good?" she asked me (they had read five of his short stories, one after the other, interspersed with "Little Earthquakes" by Tori Amos and other favorite singers of his). "He was really good, wasn't he?" I nodded, yes.

Sally called me the following Tuesday, asking me again to tell her teachers that she would be erratic in attendance, that she was going home to visit with her mother, but that she would keep up with all her written work, and please to understand. But also to thank me for coming to the memorial. Again she asked, "Wasn't he good?" I said that there was nothing to thank me for. And then she asked, "Dr. Henry, how is your son?" Which caught me off guard—I guess I had mentioned the death of children in my tragedies class, and had talked about my nine-year old David's grief in losing his best friend to cancer. I said, "He's doing better. He's trying to find new friends. But for a while, he just didn't want to participate in reality. He didn't want to go to sleep.

Didn't want to go to school." She said, "That's how I feel too."

What is happening to our kids, I wondered and wonder, still shocked. Another colleague, a stalwart, stoic 34-year-old bachelor, himself a gifted writer, explained to me that he had experimented, back when, with heroin too. That this was the other side of our generation X gap. A non-traditional, older advisee told me that heroin is everywhere, that there is a big supply of super-refined, high-grade stuff that you can sniff as powder. So pure that it does not take a needle. Around Emerson, the grapevine said, the campus cops knew all about it, but winked; heroin was commonplace. Jonathan Aaron shook his head and said, "It's telling these kids they have to write from experience, and then celebrating William Burroughs and Allen Ginsberg as saints, Saint Genet's of existentialism."

Sally Arkin graduated and moved to California, continuing her friendship with Elizabeth Searle, who told me later that Sally was now teaching young children. I can't imagine the life of that young woman, so gifted herself and intensely aware, and the burden of her grief.

SHAMROCKS AND SALAD DAYS

Seamus Heaney is a generous man by nature and by principle; perhaps sometimes too much so for his own good. He has written a humorous, yet wrenching poem about divided domestic and professional responsibilities, "An Afterwards." The poem, spoken from the viewpoint of the poet's wife, equates the poet's high-minded vocation ("who wears the bays...whose is the life most dedicated and exemplary"?) with careerism, and then mocks careerism as a sin. The poet has been damned to the ninth circle for letting books come first and not oftener walking "the twilight with me and your children." For this his punishment is to be backbitten for eternity by a rival poet, "some maker gaffs me in the neck."

But Seamus has never been a careerist, at least as I have known him. He has been like his model, W.B. Yeats, a force for living literature, a teacher and an enabler of fellow writers, whether writers of indominatable Irishry, or of international situations. Having himself earned the opportunity, he has been gladly willing to "give the other man (and woman) a hand up." He writes in the essay,

"Yeats as an Example?": "For all the activity and push of the enterprise, the aim of the poet and of the poetry is finally to be of service, to ply the effort of the individual work into the larger work of the community as a whole, and the spirit of our ages is sympathetic to that democratic urge."

His favors to *Ploughshares* literary magazine deserve particular mention, and most probably exceed the list of which I am personally aware; that is: Seamus as the subject of a feature interview by James Randall in *Ploughshares* 5/3 (along with new poems), then Seamus as guest editor of *Ploughshares* 6/1, and later again of 10/1; Seamus as the featured reader at three different fundraisers for the magazine; and finally Seamus as a trustee and then as trustee-emeritus at the point when *Ploughshares* was acquired by Emerson College. In all instances, contributor, editor, reader, and trustee, he served as an unpaid volunteer, as did we all. He honored us, I feel, in recognizing and taking part in *Ploughshares* as a collective effort "to be of service."

I first met Seamus as the friend of Peter O'Malley, who co-founded and co-directed *Ploughshares* with me, beginning in 1970; they were friends from Ireland, presumably Dublin, where Heaney had moved in 1972. Peter from the earliest days of *Ploughshares*, from its origins in the Plough and Stars pub in Cambridge (where Peter had been bartender and one of several investors in the bar), had travelled back to Dublin with copies of the magazine and sought to enlist Irish poets as contributors, among them Desmond O'Grady, John Montague, Thomas Kinsella, Hayden Murphy, Derek Mahon, and Seamus. This was during the height of the troubles between North (Seamus's native Derry and Belfast) and South (his residence in Dublin).

There had been, of course, decades of regular literary

commerce between Harvard and Dublin in overlapping careers and social circles. The writer Fanny Howe, daughter of Mark Howe (Dean of Harvard Law School) and Molly Howe (nee Manning, of Dublin), was one of the early *Ploughshares* editors and a personage in younger literary Cambridge. Molly Howe, in turn, was a passionate supporter of The Poet's Theater, and of its Irish model, founded by Yeats, The Abbey Theater. The curator of the Lamont Poetry Room at Harvard, John Sweeney, had cultivated Irish poets; as had his successors, Robert Fitzgerald and Stratis Haviaras. Robert Lowell developed a fondness for Ireland during this time. Lowell had become interested in *Ploughshares* because of Frank Bidart, his close friend, who edited an issue in 1975. Lowell and Heaney, I gathered became acquainted in Ireland; Heaney says in his 1979 *Ploughshares* interview: "anytime he was over in Ireland with Caroline in Castletown, we met them. There was a certain trust and intimacy". Heaney also admired Richard Wilbur, and Peter had married Wilbur's daughter, Ellen, just after we started *Ploughshares*.

Aside from the connection through Peter's friendship, among the earlier *Ploughshares* editors and friends, James Randall, then chairman of Emerson's writing program, had been interested in Irish poets, and had attempted to bring Heaney's friend and fellow Belfast poet, Derek Mahon to Emerson College as poet-in-residence. He had also been reading Heaney with interest and when Heaney arrived at Harvard to teach each spring semester, Randall interviewed him for *Ploughshares* 5/3, which had for its cover an original monotype portrait of Heaney by Michael Mazur; this portrait, incidentally, given its sinister leer, was variously described as "a potato with two slits," or as a portrait of Heaney as a bog person. The interview succinctly described the literary provinces of Heaney's art, and served to introduce them to ours; the substance of Heaney's "tradition," like an ambassador's portfolio, would be repeated in the first national reviews of *Field Work* and later of *Preoccupations* and *Poems 1965-1975*, first in the *New York Times Book Review*, then in *Time*. Suddenly the machinery of media recognition had smiled on Seamus and before long friends were referring to Famous Seamus.

It still seems a marvel to me how he protected the genuineness and privacy of his art, kept and has kept unswervingly to the writing, while dealing with the pressures of a visible, public career. Similarly amazing how he maintained all aspects of his integrity, as a family man, a friend, a teacher—and as an Irishman, the pride of Irish-Americans and a rallying icon for readers and nonreaders alike in venues such as the Eire Society.

At Peter's urging, Seamus agreed to edit a special "Transatlantic Issue" of *Ploughshares*, beginning in the fall of 1979. Abroad for the year, he would solicit work to represent the contemporary tradition he had described in his interview. Though the manuscript arrived late in the mails, after worried international phone calls between our first managing editor, Joyce Peseroff, and Seamus, the assemblage was remarkable. We rushed through the typesetting, proofreading, and layout, got a cover image from a book of ancient Irish art; then harangued our printer, Edwards Brothers in Ann Arbor to meet their 21 day production deadline. They proved late—subscribers, booksellers, and librarians were all querying, since here it was late May—and then finally the printer informed us that they had shipped the issue. One, two weeks passed and still it failed to arrive. We put a trace in for Roadways, the shipping company, and after another week, Roadways declared the shipment, roughly one ton of cartons stacked on three wooden skids, lost. We threatened to sue and Edwards Brothers was about to push the button for a reprint at the shipper's expense, when Road-ways declared the shipment found somewhere in Illinois. Because of the label "Ploughshares," it had been misde-livered to a farm implements wholesaler. We received it in early June and rushed to distribute copies on both sides of the Atlantic. By September, 1980, it had sold out and we were desperately hoping for returns.

From the beginning, *Ploughshares* had been working to attract new readers. Given the support from one of the first "Literary Magazine Development" grants from the NEA (1978-81), we set out to play on the cultural opposition of Irish, Catholic, and Boston College on the one side and Yankee, Protestant, and Harvard on the other. In terms of a prospective audience, this meant summoning a monied, cultural and social bloc of Irish American lawyers, doctors and businessmen, which normally remained separate from literary Boston. We mounted a benefit reading series, renting Sanders Theatre as a non-profit, and combining Robert Lowell with John McGahern, Richard Wilbur with Brian Moore, and Elizabeth Bishop with Mary Lavin (though Bishop died unexpectedly the night before and we proceeded with Friends of Bishop reading in her memo-ry). Peter then sought a downtown Boston location and organized a black-tie benefit in the Parker House, featuring his friend, Siobhan McKenna, who was touring a one-woman show, The Branchy Tree, a medley of passages from Yeats, Synge, Joyce, O'Casey and others. Though barely meeting costs, this otherwise bril-liant event did succeed in friend-raising. At a lower ticket price and in a more populist location, the Cambridge Boat House, we had standing room only for Seamus's first *Ploughshares* reading, 2/28/81, and after costs, raised more than $4500. Blocs of tickets had been underwritten by some of Peter's McKenna friends, while our earlier, literary constituencies turned out in full force.

Novelist Thomas Flanagan, who had appeared in the "Transatlantic Issue" with a rediscovery essay on Benedict Kiely, formally introduced Seamus, who stood at a music stand for lack of a podium, and with our *Ploughshares* banner behind him, began by quipping that many of us had most likely never touched a real plough, but he had, and then read from the Glanmore sonnets in *Field Work*: "Vowels ploughed into other, opened ground,/ Each verse returning like the plough turned round." A grand success. Joyce Peseroff and I had come to know Seamus directly through the editing process and he treated us with level recognition, comprehending, artist to artist, I felt, as we comprehended apart from and behind the social commotion.

Our friends, patrons, readers, all lamented and yet romanticized the element of sacrifice in perpetuating *Ploughshares*, how it operated always on a shoestring. By 1984, the year, finally I was hired full-time at Emerson, my first and only full-time, paid job, the shoestring both for Peter and for me had frayed to a filament. Life was catching up with us, marriages, children. Seamus, firmly ensconced at Harvard as the Boylston Professor, was in Cambridge that year, and had edited for us long distance again, this time an issue selected entirely from unsolicited work, 10/1: "Occasionally," he wrote in his introduction, "the plough broke new ground, but its usual work was to plough up the old ground and criss-cross its own furrows." He invited Peter and me to his quarters in Adams House, and we talked about somehow getting Boston College to sponsor the magazine. I said something at the time to Peter about my having "gotten my nut, but you still have to get yours," meaning some form of full-time livelihood. And I remember Seamus's sharp glance.

In the next few years, the toll of lives put Peter and me increasingly at odds. Operating primarily on public grants, we had been obliged to organize, legally, not as a partnership, but as a charity, with the two of us as co-directors overseen by trustees. The trustees were, after a fashion, Peter's friends, Bernard McCabe (critic and former English Department chairperson at Tufts, who admired Peter's musical compositions), Daniel Aaron (close friend of Peter's father-in-law, Richard Wilbur), and Barry Spacks (also a Wilbur friend, for some years in absentia in California). Seamus agreed informally to join this number, but had not as yet been formally elected.

Meanwhile, Emerson College was seeking to negotiate an affiliation. They had been subsidizing my volunteer time in operating the magazine by granting me course releases, and the writing program, as created by James Randall, already overlapped with the *Ploughshares* community.

Peter had come in and met with me and the new Writing Division Chair, Richard Duprey, and had behaved cordially, saying that the *Ploughshares* board would like a formal letter of interest from Emerson, which Duprey promptly sent. Then Peter dropped out of touch for nearly a year, while I continued to build the fiscal base and operations of the magazine; and while, at Emerson, Duprey having moved to fill a vacancy as Acting Graduate Dean, I worked as Acting Chair of the Writing Division, and the President pressured me directly for progress on the *Ploughshares* matter.

Some time before, the magazine had moved from my second bedroom into a rented store front office nearby in Watertown. The budget had grown enough to support our first managing editor, Joyce Peseroff, who had been coming in two or three times a week for $4000. When after two years, she left to write, teach, and to start a family, she was followed by Suzannah Lee, for $6000, and then by Jennifer Rose, who boosted the job to $9000. Each managing editor, working day by day with me, became another witness to the realities of how *Ploughshares* survived and operated.

I called and left messages for Peter, and as the urgency mounted of a grant report to be signed, or an application, or some corporate document, I might catch him for a moment at his apartment in Cambridge, but we rarely spoke or met. I wrote to him, finally, that we needed to reply to the College's statement of interest in *Ploughshares* before the end of June, 1987. He had by this time promised to consult with his friend, John Taylor Williams, as our pro bono attorney, and to send the college a letter. But the promised letter never arrived and at the end of July, I wrote him: "We can't keep not communicating and are overdue with a businesslike response to Emerson." By mid-August, I wrote him tersely that I assumed his silence constituted consent and that I was going forward with the business of the organization. I would keep him informed. By November, in a friendly tone, I wrote him in an update: "the next emergency is to sit down with the lawyers and worked our a reorganization that will allow us to proceed with corporate fundraising and/or affiliation." Again, we needed to expand the board, and "we have to address the reality of how the organization operates and can operate in the future..." I didn't see "the co-directorship as a reality," and recommended a true overseeing board of a trustees and an Executive Director. *Ploughshares* couldn't survive another year if we continued "begging or ignoring these issues." Still no response from Peter.

At this point, I tried contacting our trustees, Daniel

Aaron, Bernard McCabe, Barry Spacks, and Seamus. McCabe was in England, Spacks in California, but Aaron and Heaney were both at Harvard. Seamus met me for lunch, and after hearing my concerns, suggested that I write to McCabe, which I did. Then Seamus met me again to go over the draft of my letter, and to soften its rancor. I outlined the *Ploughshares* situation as honestly as I could, appealing now to the trustees because Peter had been absent and had refused to resolve issues central to the survival of the magazine. I described earlier attempts to expand the board, which Peter appeared to view as a move to "get him out." I described my frustration at Peter's unilateral actions in the name of *Ploughshares* in matters where I would have had an opinion and informed concern, namely his earlier approaches to Boston College and Brown. Now we had a letter from Emerson, which called for a response.

McCabe wrote back, agreeing that *Ploughshares* faced an administrative crisis and offered to come over in May for an "extraordinary meeting of the trustees." I sent a memo to all parties, including Peter, again detailing our problems, and, with Seamus's generous help, calling for a meeting at Seamus's house at 10 Kirkland Place on May 8. The afternoon of the meeting was sunny and humid. Seamus and his wife, Marie, offered everyone drinks. After our official meeting, we would have a gracious sit-down dinner. Bernard, Dan Aaron, Seamus, and Peter spoke casually about Irish composers and about the tenor, John O'Sullivan, whose music Seamus was playing from a tape. Eventually we stepped out onto a screened in porch with a long dining table, where places had been set, each with a yellow pad and pencil, a xeroxed agenda (handwritten by Seamus), and a glass of water. Ellen Wilbur, as Clerk, kept the minutes. We managed to settle the resignation by phone of Barry Spacks, and the election of Seamus, and of Peter's lawyer friend, Ike Williams, also called by phone from the meeting, as new trustees. We all promised to submit additional suggestions for later action. McCabe was Chairperson of the trustees. Seamus and Bernard would write a letter from the trustees to Emerson; Ike Williams would serve pro-bono as the *Ploughshares* counsel.

The trustees' letter was sent the next day to Emerson and replied to now by John Zacharis, as Emerson's Senior Vice President. He wrote back that he had hired "a consulting attorney for the college," Jim Samels, to draft some ideas for achieving "greater exposure for the college" in sponsoring *Ploughshares*, without the college assuming part-ownership or control of the magazine.

Samels began meeting with me in the fall of 1988. I met with Peter in September in a restaurant on Charles Street. He told me that Bernard and Seamus (back in Dublin at this point) were coming over later in the fall and I should write them that the Emerson proposal was forthcoming. If the deal went through, Peter said he would sever his connection with the magazine. That he was hiring a lawyer, and I should too, to "determine a settlement of his personal interests."

Samels was manic, eccentric and tenacious. Zacharis had chosen him, given Peter's stalling, for his street smarts. He would call me at any hour at home, asking for ideas, responses to ideas, and pressing me for progress reports. Often he called on his car phone, which would go dead as he drove through a tunnel or overpass; often, grunting with exertion, he would call from his exercise bike. He seemed amused by my mendicant idealism and enjoyed boasting of his own good life for contrast. Despite his fast talking, high pressure manner, I believed he understood the special value of *Ploughshares*, and that he promised the only realistic, foreseeable resolution to the *Ploughshares* wars, short of killing the magazine. The proposal we discussed was for a trial year, leading to a full-scale "buy-out" rather than a sponsorship. By early January, 1989, Emerson was proposing a $30,000 cash subvention in exchange for presence on the *Ploughshares* board, free advertising, and the addition of "at Emerson College" to our logos. Then at the end of the year, Emerson would have first refusal on a "buy out," perhaps in the $100,000 range, which would go towards an endowment. Faculty course releases could help fund staff positions. Jennifer Rose at this point submitted a friendly letter of resignation, and I hired my former student Don Lee in her place, "since he has been gradually groomed to that role."

At Emerson, Richard Duprey had returned as Division Chair and my application for tenure was being reviewed—strictly a separate issue from the *Ploughshares* negotiations, I was told. I was distressed by a split vote in the faculty, but by March my tenure had been granted. Samels met alone with Peter in early May. Emerson was pressing for a resolution that could be announced at graduation. Peter made verbal demands that echoed his earlier claims; he was seeking a continuing salary and a title as well as a pay off. He stalled well past the graduation deadline, then finally sent a letter in which he claimed that the *Ploughshares* trustees were his appointees; that he had the "sole authority to represent *Ploughshares*"; that we already had two other offers of affiliation; that he had "led" the magazine for twenty years; and that in any deal, all editorial decisions must be the province of "the editors, DeWitt Henry and Peter O'Malley," and that he, Peter, must be acknowledged "as working head of the magazine." When Samels asked for my response, I suggested designating Peter as "Founding Publisher" on the masthead; I also conceded to a fifty/fifty split of up to $15,000 settlement for work in the past, an amount to be raised only from the sale of back inventory. Samels replied formally to Peter with these terms, as well as with the substance of Emerson's proposal (which was a pledge of $250,000 over a five year period in exchange for a full transfer of *Ploughshares*'s assets and rights to Emerson). Peter again stalled.

In the meantime, on the Emerson front, Duprey resigned as Division Chair, effective August 1; he supported my appointment as Chair, and the faculty duly approved.

In July I wrote my own ultimatum to our trustees. I was ready to resign and, if necessary, start a new magazine at Emerson, unless: 1) I was empowered as Executive Director, 2) I served in a well-organized structure, overseen by a working board, 3) we had means to support paid staff and to continue building our fiscal base. As I understood the Emerson proposal, it accommodated these conditions. In addition, as tenured faculty and as incoming Chair of the Writing division, I was in a position to make much more possible than these terms alone suggested. I then contacted Heaney, Aaron, and McCabe separately by phone and learned that none of them had heard of or seen Emerson's letter of June 30 to Peter until it arrived appended by me to my memo; that each now approved of the Emerson proposal; and that Seamus and Bernard would send personal letters to Peter to that effect.

Things got crazier and crazier. I had a call at home from one Gerald Gross, a Vice President at BU, who said he was a friend of Richard Wilbur and of Ike Williams, and that he hoped to meet with me to discuss BU's acquisition of *Ploughshares*. I said flatly that the trustees of *Ploughshares* had already approved of an arrangement with Emerson, and any further discussion concerning

BU would be inappropriate. Samels and I now did some investigating, and when it became clear that Gerald Gross was serious, that Peter had spoken with him, that my friend Sven Birkerts had been called in for a meeting and offered the salaried Executive Director position (Birkerts called to tell me he had turned it down), that Gross so far was acting on his own and had not yet approached Silber, that no one in the English Department or Creative Writing Program had yet been consulted, and that the endowment figure being proposed by Gross was one million dollars; when all this became clear, Samels then threatened to sue BU for "interference with Emerson's advantageous relationship with *Ploughshares*." Negotiations were dropped. Internally, Gross was embarrassed. Later, in mid-September, Ike Williams sent a formal letter to the *Ploughshares* Trustees, angrily resigning. He explained that in his limited, pro-bono role as an advisor, given Emerson's lack of assurance of tenure for me and its hype about using *Ploughshares* to build a commercial writing program, he had encouraged Peter "to test the waters at BU." He did not like "being bullied and threatened"; did not like "my friends and clients being bullied and threatened"; did not approve of the Emerson proposal.

Since Bernard McCabe was in London and Seamus now in Dublin, Dan Aaron in his Harvard office served to represent the will of the trustees and was given power of attorney. As friends to Peter, all parties were distressed by their involvement, yet all remained generously concerned and responsible. Samels met with Dan Aaron. Dan then conferred with Seamus and Bernard by transatlantic phone, and on September 20 the three of them agreed to accept the Emerson proposal.

Once the transfer was official, I wrote to Ellen that I was sorry for the strife that *Ploughshares* had caused.

There was no answer at the time, and neither she nor Peter appeared at our inaugural *Ploughshares* at Emerson party, January 22, 1990, to celebrate "the journal's contribution to contemporary letters, its new status as an Emerson publication, and its aspirations for the Nineties."

Peter and I had no contact. I heard that he was separating from Ellen. He signed his first *Ploughshares* check from Emerson over to Ellen. Once the *Ploughshares* office had moved to campus, he called Don Lee and stopped in to collect a full back file of the magazine. I ran into him there and we had a cordial exchange. Having separated from Ellen, he had an apartment with a bay window right across from O Marlborough, the Emerson dorm where I now went for lunch. He traveled a lot, and had another apartment in Munich. He'd come into some money. He had a German partner in Munich and they were acquiring rights to foreign films for distribution in the U.S. They'd just bought the rights to Felix the Cat. I helped carry the boxed back issues out to the front of the building, so he could come around and load them into his car.

In connection with Associated Writing Programs, I staged and used the *Ploughshares* friendships to stage a benefit reading entitled "Love Sick" on Valentine's Day, 1990. As we had in the heyday of *Ploughshares* benefits, Stratis Haviaras helped me to enlist Seamus as a reader and the Sanders Theatre rental. The readers besides Seamus were Gerry Stern, Jayne Anne Phillips, Grace Paley, and Sharon Olds. We had a terrific turnout. Seamus's favor, however, was to Stratis and to me personally. He was finished otherwise in any connection with *Ploughshares*, partly out of deference to Peter's feelings, partly out of having done his turn. He'd had enough, thank you.

In mid-March, the *Ploughshares* trustees officially resigned and elected Jim McPherson, Carol Smith, and Frank Bidart as their successors.

Shortly thereafter, late in the spring, 1990, Seamus read with Dick Wilbur at Harvard to benefit Stratis's Woodberry Poetry Room. I bought my ticket and I sat high up in the Sanders Audience with a sad, sad sense of *deja vu* and dissociation. There was Peter in the front row, as if he had organized everything. From my distance: there my friends, there the literary mob, there Ellen, there Peter and Ellen's son, Gabriel. Our association of twenty years was over. We weren't speaking. A few left over old time *Ploughshares* patrons, like guests from Gatsby's parties showing up after his death, apparently still hadn't heard, and thought this was a *Ploughshares* event. Others avoided hellos, eye contact, or any evidence of *Ploughshares* solidarity.

My last sight of Peter was after we had moved to 180 Tremont and I was still Chairperson. I was walking back from an early appointment at Emerson's administrative building along Newbury and caught sight of him having breakfast presumably at a sidewalk table at 29 Newbury, a stylish bar and restaurant. He was reading Variety. He wore dark glasses and had moussed his hair to look like Robert DiNero. I didn't stop and he didn't see me.

My last sight of Seamus and of Marie Heaney was at a benefit reading at Radcliffe several years ago for The Poets' Theatre, organized by a former *Ploughshares* editor and friend, David Gullette. Seamus read with John McGahern. We all had aged, but in the midst of distraction, he fixed me with a look of instant comprehension, woe, and measure—a ninth circle look—pressing my hand: "How are you," he asked.

THE SAGA OF A CHAIR

The fake-leather reading chair, as listed on Target's website, was made in China. I imagine a factory for mass-produced, upholstered furniture: chairs, ottomans, sofas. And this chair conceived of and designed for customer assembly. Imagine the supplies. The waterproof and durable fabric. The sponge rubber stuffing. The metal parts and wooden parts. How they are boxed and stock-piled.

The standardized product, produced on demand, and shipped. A factory like my father's candy factory, a warehouse, a shipping dock; the salesmen and marketing operations; the semitrailer rigs at the shipping dock; boxes of disassembled chairs stacked on skids, the skids carried by electric lifts and into the truck; the truck to train perhaps, the train to waterfront harbor, container freight, ocean voyage, unloading in San Francisco, trucked to Target's warehouse, then by more trucks to Target's chain countrywide, and to Boston, to Watertown. So many hands, so many languages, so many miles; so many lives!

For my son Dave's senior year at Emerson, after determined apartment hunting on his part, we moved him into an apartment in Boston's North End, at the end of Hanover Street near City Hall. This meant learning a new part of town for me, in the many trips in my Ford Focus hatchback, double-parked on the narrow, busy street, with high-toned restaurants on both sides, valet parkers, and depending on the time of day or night, throngs of revelers and tourists. As usual with moves, our compact car was burdened with regular-sized boxspring and mattress (better than any in our home) on the roof, and the hatch stuffed with bins of electronics, boots, shoes, coats, shirts—everything Dave referred to as "his life." He had picked out a desk for sophomore year. He insisted on plastic bins with lids for packing (rather than boxes).

Connie had found the apartment with him and I had only heard about it, hard wood floors, $1400 per month, and Dave had found a friend Pete to share the rent.

I thought now, having dipped into a special trust account we had started years before, and used the money to buy a $1000 HD flat screen TV for Dave; having gotten Connie to buy a special stand for the monster at Target; having gotten me to buy a bed-frame for his box-spring, I now heard that he wanted a leather chair for his room, brown leather. He insisted that it be new. They sold them at Target also, for $300. Connie and he dragged me along to look at them.

We shopped around, compared prices and chairs on the web, and when Dave and I went to buy—me grumbling about the price and wondering how and whether it would fit in my car and how we would manage to unload it on the other end, given the traffic (I did think to apologize for my negative thinking and Dave said, good, just stop it)–the Target in Watertown was out of stock. We checked back a few more times, same story. School started.

Then I found the chair, brown leather, on Target on line, with free delivery. Dave didn't want it delivered to him because he wouldn't be home, between his classes and looking for work. Okay, in 48 hours, I had it delivered to our house in Watertown. I came home from teaching in the afternoon and there it was in back, in the driveway, a box at least 4x4x4 feet. I managed, just, to get it inside my hatchback, though I could barely see behind me in sideview mirrors. My daughter and I drove it in that night around 11:30, and actually found a space across from the apartment. Called Dave's cell. He and Pete came down and excitedly we lugged it out and into his apartment foyer, up the stairs, slid it down the hall and into his open doorway: a kitchen! Pete's room to left, Dave's to right.

We attacked the box. Pete had a screw driver and hammer and we assembled the chair, so. But as soon as Ruth and I got home, Dave had called Connie and said it was the *wrong* chair. He wanted me to take it home with the box, which I did, keeping it in our shed, while I tried to get the correct chair and figure how to get it. I checked on line, but sale items had changed. The correct chair in brown was discounted to $299, but now had a $75 delivery charge; yet a week later, it was offered with such a deep discount, that even with the shipping charge it was $250. I ordered it, and when it arrived at home, I drove the new chair in its box to Dave's. Back home, I made a separate trip to Target, armed with an online return form, with the old chair. I loaded it into a shopping cart, along with the panels of the broken box, and wheeled it in to the returns counters, where I got immediate attention and $299 credited back to my account, deed done. I felt efficient and proud that the saga of the chair had ended happily.

Weeks passed and Dave was happy in his chair, which I still hadn't seen in situ, when I got a ticket in the mail at home from the Boston trash patrol for $1000 for illegal dumping (the city's ordinance against non-residents). Dave had left the second box for trash pickup and it had had my name and address on it. He argued that he and Pete had put it out on the city's scheduled trash day, but that either the collection must have come earlier than usual, or later, and that in the meantime an officer had spotted the address label. I made this argument in my best prose in protesting the ticket, and we got a court date for Friday, December 14, at 1pm.

There was snow. I headed to Emerson, parked in my underground garage space, and called Dave to meet me at 24 Chardon Street, the court building across from City Hall. Took the subway to Government Center, then walked a couple of blocks to the immense Edward Brooke Courthouse. Inside, I went up modern stairs in an open courtyard to the 3rd floor and a busy office that looked like the Registry. I waited for Dave, called him on my cell for his progress. It was almost 1pm and he was still walking. I graded papers in the meantime. Finally I went into the main desk alone, where a clerk told me to stand in line. As I waited, Dave arrived and stood with me. Each person, in turn, was called inside a door, then after a few minutes came out again, smiling. At last it was our turn. One officer welcomed us in and another sat with papers at a table. We all sat down.

"Tell us your story," the greeter said, after they find the right number of the ticket.

I explained that there are two hearing notices, in error. They hadn't yet read my appeal. "Just tell us," the desk officer said. So Dave jumped in, succinctly. "I live at 224 Hanover. My dad bought me a chair for my birthday —." I added that it came in a big box, as Dave continued: "And I broke down the box and put it out for trash collection on trash day. It had my dad's name and address on the label." No questions. "Dismissed," the captain said, in spirit of the holidays. We thanked them and left.

I was disappointed that no one had read my letter, but proud that Dave had taken over and reduced it to straight talk over my stammering. We took the T back to campus and someone on his cell invited Dave to lunch (and then his class). I went back to my office.

⁂ ⁂ ⁂

At Emerson, Jerald Walker became the Writing, Literature, Publishing Department Chairperson, a post I had held several years before his hire. He furnished the chairperson's office with two of these Target chairs, brown, fake leather, and all too familiar to me, as we sat and cordially discussed workloads.

I am long since retired. Dave finished his MA in Marketing at Emerson, then moved to Manhattan to hunt for internships. Eventually he found work as an UX designer; settled into an international marketing firm, and was promoted. Met and married Judy, moved to a Hoboken condo and became a Dad himself. He wanted nothing to do with used furnishings and their tastes ran to Ikea. The brown chair, left with us, remains my favorite, though after regular use, much of its leather veneer on the seat and arms has worn away, revealing tan cloth.

AN AFFAIR TO REMEMBER

Sure, sure, we've got the star personalities of Kerr and Grant for starters (both English, both elegantly mannered, with a distancing wit perfectly poised with wholehearted passion: Grant here will play the same charm he played in, say, Hitchcock's *To Catch a Thief* or in *Bringing Up Baby* with Katherine Hepburn; Kerr will play her repressed yet passionate *King and I* self).

Now for situation. We want the tension of adultery, of socially forbidden love, but a 1950's mass audience will not celebrate adultery. We will tease the idea, to be sure, by using the word "affair" in the title. But let's try this set up: both characters are engaged to publicly known rich fiances, while both themselves are relatively hardscrable and incompetent to earn a living (let's make them both talented, but shy artists, she as a singer, he as a painter). We won't press the matter, but both are freeloaders, planning to marry for money, social status, and security. The conflict, then, is that they fall in love, partly thanks to their ability to see through each other; two charmers charm each other; but if they indulge their love on ship board, like adulterous lovers, they will be witnessed and judged by society and lose their rich fiances and marital prospects. Let's have them choose to pursue their true natures, not impetuously, but passionately. They will separate for six months, break with their fiances, and work hard separately as artists to earn a living. In other words, they give each other the purpose and confidence to fulfill their individual natures. Then they are to meet, compare notes, and marry. But, let's see, what larger, O'Henry-ish obstacle can we contrive? Got it! How about if just as She is going to meet Him and is "looking up," She is hit by a car, so He is left with the idea that she has decided against their marrying and has broken her promise. Yeah, yeah, the story can get away with this; cheap shot, yeah, but we're not talking witty reparte anymore, we're talking Love in the Hands of Fate (or perhaps an Angry God).

This is pure O'Henry: she sells her hair to buy him a watch fob, while he sells his watch to buy her a comb. When she comes to in the hospital, having almost died, she discovers that she may not walk again, or at least for more than a year. Let's have the local priest in there, ostensibly to offer her last rites, but as she comes out of her coma and looks as if she may recover, at least as a physically challenged person, let's have the priest like her and find her a socially redeeming job, even if she is confined to a wheelchair. Meanwhile, let her decide, projecting in her mind how Mr Right must have interpreted her not showing up to marry, not to let Mr Right know otherwise. Why? She doesn't want to burden him with concern for her handicap, or with concern for paying her medical bills; she still has to prove her independent ability to support herself and to find social purpose for herself, apart from romance. So she does. She manages. She will eventually be able to walk.

But still, maybe now for fear of appearing less desirable, what?, she doesn't contact Him, and it is only by (divine) accident, that on her first night out with her ex-fiancé and good friend, she meets Him in a way—both are attending a concert, a celebration of High Art that conceals her handicap—and he still sees her as a traitor to their Love. But then his beloved Aunt dies and leaves Her the lace shawl, so He makes the initiative of contact, looks her up in the phonebook, and barges into her apartment (where conveniently she is lying on the couch, legs covered) and intending bitterness, delivers the shawl. But in parting, He sees Her as the vision of parting or greeting he has painted with memory and imagination, his best painting, which his agent says a crippled young woman has bought. Aha! Let the light bulb turn on! It was her! She must be crippled! That must be why she didn't make the rendezvous! He pushes into her bedroom and there is the painting! Oh Art! Oh Love! Oh Providence, not Fate! We'll have them weeping in the aisles. He'll see it all in one wrenching recognition, fist to forehead. He'll paint, and she will walk again (and presumably sing standing up), and they will love forever and ever and prosper and enrich the world with the mutual art and their children and their children's art! Roll credits. Yes. Here's my five million. Let's make it! Sure thing! But it's got to be Kerr and Grant, not, please your classic marrieds, Donna Reed and Jimmy Stewart *(It's A Wonderful Life),* and not your classic adulterers, Burt Lancaster and Deborah Kerr *(From Here to Eternity).*

A TRIBUTE TO "TORNADO AT THE CLUB," FROM EVAN S. CONNELL'S MRS. BRIDGE

—1—

Mr. Bridge

I determined a special occasion to surprise India with the steamship tickets for the grand tour, Rome, Florence, Venice. We had planned on dinner at the Kansas City Country Club, itself a special occasion in our routines. We drove there in good weather, though there was some prediction of a storm; I know my weather, nevertheless, having lived in Kansas man and boy now for 58 years. I saw no cause for alarm. The waiter, although distracted, showed us to our usual table. I saw Heinrich Auslander, the psychiatrist, brazen in public with his young mistress at the corner table. Muriel and her husband were across the room. The lamb roast appealed to me and I ordered it for both India and myself. In my pocket nestled the tickets, my surprise. When our plates came, no sooner had we begun eating, when the waiter came over and said something about a tornado. The radio, he said, was advising shelter. Well, I thought, there is no need for panic. No need to spoil an appointed evening, one that I had planned so definitely. The winds outside were high, but not alarming. The rain was heavy. It would pass by. These storms usually did. This club had stood here for a good two generations. True disasters by tornado were exaggerated and improbable. But people were alarmist. They enjoyed alarm. I have no truck with alarm. One, two, three, then all the patrons lost their nerve and headed like cattle for the club shelter. The waiter came and begged us to accompany them. He was polite, despite his scared eyes and manner, eager himself to escape. I told him, No, No, thank you. We will stay here. That is my philosophy. And that is India's philosophy as my wife. She is a sweet, good woman, though given to childishness. She asked me whether the girl with Heinrich was his daughter and I had to laugh, saying "Not exactly," and she smiled and shied from the impropriety. Heinrich himself tapped at my shoulder on his way out and said with evident sarcasm, which I pretended to ignore, "Quite the Napoleon, eh Walter?" I have no truck with the likes of him. He doesn't even belong in our club, except for his money. I saw that India was growing alarmed. I wanted to reassure her as I always do in the world by insisting on my own credit that nothing was out of the normal. Even if it wasn't, even if we were in the slightest danger, I felt it was more important to shelter her with her trust in me, than to subject her to distress. I asked for butter, which she got up to steal from a deserted table. Outside the lawn furniture was blown against the window. The lights went out. "India," I said, pulling out my envelope. "Here is a surprise birthday present for you." Sitting across from me, loyally paying mind only to me despite her evident worry about the storm, she took the envelope and opened it and astonished delight illuminated her lovely face. Tickets to Europe! Steamship tickets and the trains, from Rome to Venice to Florence. We would have, now that the children were grown, our long awaited honeymoon. At that moment the storm had passed. The lights came on. "India," I said, "have I ever been wrong?"

—2—
The Waiter

I'd been listening to the radio. Tornado watch! Heading this way! 75 miles per hour! I don't like to alarm the guests; a false alarm to these people could cost my job, but so could ignoring real danger. And me, I'm a careful man myself. I'll do my job with the best, but I'm scared myself and from what the radio says, it's high time to head for shelter. I go to each table and tell each party. Tornado warning. We are closing the dining room just to be safe. Outside the wind was strong and sky dark as dusk, driving rain. Lawn furniture was turning over and blowing—one chair hit the French doors. The Iversons, the Smythes, the Daggots, all got up, leaving their elegant meals, napkins on their chairs, to hurry out, orderly fashion. I was edgy to follow them. This was too big a storm, too fast, heading right on top of us. If it hit us with the funnel this whole establishment would suck to kindling, fancy clientele or not. But some of these people, that Doctor Heinrich and his lady, he just sat there calm as anything by the window watching the others. Then thank goodness he got up. I went over to the other party, Mr. and Mrs. Bridge. I tried to warn them politely, like I wasn't too scared, but I was doing my duty and a man has to look out for himself in the face of catastrophe. I told them, Folks, there isn't much time. That funnel is going to hit here any minute. Please, Mr. Bridge, we are asking the guests to wait it over in the basement shelter. Mrs. Bridge heard me and that was a frightened lady. Her eyes were wide. She was looking behind me at the clatter of lawn furniture and the sideways rain and sudden ripping of the dining room awnings clear off in the wind. But that Mr. Bridge just smiled up at me, chewing his lamb roast, mouth too full to speak and made the smile and wink to say, Thomas, my man, the lamb roast is excellent, excellent! I said, I told him, I can't stay, I can't stay, folks. Please come! Then I turned and I saw that huge funnel cloud real as life, and it was filling the sky. The Doctor Heinrich was watching and urging his girlfriend there, when he stopped by the Bridges' table. I heard him laugh and say, "Such a brave man, your husband is, Mrs. Bridge!" Then laughing he joined his girl, thank goodness, and he was hurrying alongside me, though I let them go down first, and I followed. The lights were out. I had the emergency flashlight shining for them. Those Bridges! He was my witness. I warned them all I could. I did my duty to the last and I was risking my life for that Bridge man's bravery, if that's what you can call such craziness. That man is crazy. That man's wife is crazy, staying with him too. And both them crazy rich or not are going to be blown off God's earth, while this brave man, brave enough and sensible enough too, did his level best to the last for their good. But comes a time, a man's life is his own, to stay or go. Listen to that! Down here with all the people now. Lanterns lit. All close here huddled and joking. And that doctor lighting his cigar, joking, "That Walter Bridge. Why he's like one of Napoleon's fourteen year old foot soldiers." But I pray for us all. Please God, let us live. Save us from your wrath, Lord, and save us from the fools among us too. Amen.

—3—

The Tornado

I was following my nature, gathering energy, building up to a forward vector at 75 miles per hour. I roared and churned and spun, my funnel twisting down from the strength of storm cloud, rain, lightning. My funnel crossed farmland, sucking dirt and crops. It tore up fences and trees and telephone and electric lines and drove and danced and meandered, mocking and teaching the earth—which is me too; we are all one thing. Houses, barns, cars, animals, all churned into my vacuum, lifted and spun into my heart. I cut across the outskirts of the city, through crowded neighborhoods and roads and factories and drove on over hills, craving, seeking, like history itself, like war, the juggernaut of happening past resistance. Out of my way, survivors! Hide in cellars! Try to outrun and dodge my path! Take shelter! I want you. There. There, ahead, the country club. Exclusive. The rolling fairways and landscaped greens. But then the clubhouse. Lights shining in my darkness. Fragile lawn furniture. Awnings flapping. I want them. My winds seek and test and tear. And inside now the lights go out. Man efforts to make light. Man shelters. And there sit two diners, openly exposed, denying my power. The Bridges, Walter and India. I rattle the French doors. I rain and pelt and roar. I tear the awning clear off. But inside they ignore me. They match my very force with their denial. I don't exist. They don't care if I do exist. I feel the pure insistence of their eating. They don't care if I tear the roof off the club and I suck them out of their chairs. I believe if they were in my winds, if they spun in my funnel upside down or sideways, still they would keep the posture of sitting, even without chairs. Still they would talk, even if they were separated, the other somewhere out of sight above or below. The force of their intentness not only equals, it defies mine, I confess. It turns me aside. My funnel misses them. I am lessening, even as I pass towards that horizon, over those trees. I spread into the sky.

FACE TO FACE

My 74-year-old self reads and republishes my 24-year-old self in *Falling: Six Stories*. Would my 24-year-old self be impressed by, learn from, or recognize his own writing dreams in the work of 74? Would we embarrass each other?

The world should sing, 24 writes. There's no point telling ugliness. His love is Faulkner, especially *As I Lay Dying*. I'll sacrifice my life for art, he vows. Pent up in a stuffy attic room with his typewriter, a rocking chair, and a window air-conditioner, as well as with Faulkner, he reads Aeschylus, Euripides and Sophocles in translation. He writes slowly, revising as he goes until each increment seems final. He reads Frost's dramatic monologues. Two of his favorite moments in this story, "Lord of Autumn": one character's swallowing egg yolk in the midst of other characters' anxieties; and the matriarch's agonized waiting for news, touching her forehead to the screen. The two most difficult moments: the patriarch's fall with the running horse (from which 24 cribbed both from Tolstoy and Hemingway), and the son's cradling his fallen father in the bed of a speeding pick-up.

A longer, looser version of this passed as his college thesis, the second ever allowed at Amherst College. Encouraged by an editor at Doubleday, it was the subject of a reader's report that broke 24's heart at the time, but which he treasured. "The author is a very sensitive writer, and he describes everything....He is in love with life. But the reader gets bogged down in these details...Still the novel does have a sort of super-real, heightened aware-ness, which makes it almost unreal. It is haunting. It reminds me of a European one-act play...But I wish the author would break away from this tightness, his very structure, and write more directly, more passionately." In college, he had changed his ambition from Steinbeckian thickness to a lyrical and ironic understatement. He had learned irony, for better of worse. When Richard Yates read his sample at Iowa in 1966, he said okay you've done this, I know who you are, now let's move on. Yates disliked Faulkner stories.

We all have had the experience, somewhat, in viewing photographs and films/videos of ourselves from decades before. You remember inhabiting that kid, remember posing for that snapshot. All my memories in my memoir, *Sweet Dreams* (2001, when 60): time, place, circumstance.

Likewise, in aging, at 30th reunions for high school and college, we enter a room full of seeming strangers, seeking for resemblances to our graduation selves at 18, at 22. We wear our name tags.

Imagine now, instead of seeing yourself at 74, your daily face in the mirror, the face you shave, floss, brush teeth, the face whose eyes you stare into sometimes with perfect, tragic understanding, indeed the only face you can stare into and fully know what thoughts and feelings inhabit it...like and not like Narcissus.....imagine instead that what looks back at you is your face at five, ten, fourteen, eighteen.

Good God, are you *me*? both selves exclaim, horrified.

Faces bloom, then bloat, or wizen and wither. Bodies thicken, soften, and stoop. Selves lurk, lost in a clutter of flesh, costumes and roles. At 50th high school reunions we peer at former classmates for recognition: where are you, Judy Stradley, inside there? Where Lil Kemp? We see the changes in our children. The photos remind us of their childhood's phases, more treasured by us now than by them (funny if not humiliating for them). For once, the living faces stop, some instant captured. There's the life mask of Abe Lincoln in the Huntington Museum, Pasadena; the shock of the real man. The sculpture my wife Connie's father made of her face at eight, which drifts around our home now, even as our two granddaughters dash, cry, play, sing, exploring artifacts like brigands. (I had thought it was a life mask, but when I asked if she remembered having him grease her face, then lay on wet plaster, she'd said no. She remembered posing. Remembered his studying her face intently and working with the clay.) We save our children's baby teeth. Locks of soft, dark hair. I have a rolled and yellowed birth certificate now that I remember my mother keeping in the bank's deposit box, and it shows my infant footprints.

Technologies of preservation change. From drawings and oil portraits (by and of), to snapshots and portraits to digital photos and videos. Old movies, VHS tapes. My sister Judy is Judy. Connie is Connie. I am me. There is the startle of transformations, but the constancies also.

Then, now, for keeps. What stays. What's lost.

Tillie Olsen, on a grander scale, earned classic status for her stories, *Tell Me A Riddle* (1961); then published her apprentice novel from the Thirties, *Yonnandio: From The Thirties* (1974) late in life.

THOUGHTS ON TILLIE OLSEN,
WRITER, TEACHER, ACTIVIST

Yonnondio: From the Thirties, published by Seymour Lawrence/Delacorte in 1974, was Olsen's unfinished first novel (set aside when she was twenty-four), and reads like Zola or Steinbeck lyricized. There's an explicit radical purpose (a framework of proletarian exhortation), constant injustice and defeat, and society to blame, and heroisms of endurance, imagination, and spiritual resilience. The family involved begins in the coal fields (the opening chapter was published originally in one of the earliest issues of *The Partisan Review*), flees capitalistic oppression there for a tenant farm, enjoys a brief idyll of life in nature only once again to be defeated by the owner taking everything, and finally ends up in the city, where the father works first in a slaughter house, then in sewering, then nothing. The focus throughout is on the mother, Anna, who suffers all, breaks, gets sick, goes mad, yet comes back and endures, and on the daughter, Mazie, who is all unspoiled potential, and who might somehow get out of it, physically, imaginatively, and I suppose like Olsen herself go on to bear the responsibility for those who couldn't and have not. But the book stops before there's any real promise of Mazie's escape, and the last line is Anna's: "I see for it to end tomorrow....get tolerable."

It *is* a 30's book and I think if it had been published in 1934 it might now be required reading; and some readers will embrace or dismiss it as such—a relic of naturalism in a Marxist frame. It's also an interesting, moving, beautifully written and occasionally beautiful novel, for then or now. But most importantly it's a kind of missing link to the character and intensity of Olsen herself, and as she embodies the partisans vs. artist conflict that Daniel Aaron described in *Writers on the Left.* I think of Aaron's quoting Sherwood Anderson's defense of *Winesburg, Ohio* as his most "revolutionary" book, and asking that writers like him should be left free to explore "deeper facts" without resort to propaganda.

As I see Olson's progress from this novel to *Tell Me A Riddle* (1961), either she heeds Anderson's example or 1950's censorship was a healthy thing for her art, and by inhibiting her overt partisanship, freed the artist. She still is a writer on the Left in these wonderful stories, especially in "Oh, Yes," and "Tell Me A Riddle" (her best —anyone's best), but you have to look closely to realize it. She's worked past easy protest to the internal complexities of character—its mystery, life's mystery (and "mystery" itself signals the switch of emphasis); forces of constriction and defeat are more permeating and vague and hence imaginatively accessible; protest is down, and sympathy, comedy, and sad wonder up. *That* writer is present in the earlier book too, for otherwise it would be unbearable; but is deflected by the frame. So much seems to be pathetic or an outrageous example that there isn't time to worry about the fullness of people. The conflict persists in her mind and career, including her essays on Rebecca Harding Davis's *Life in the Iron Mills* and an excerpt from *Requa* (*Best American Short Stories*, 1971), a work in progress: how to reconcile the historical-political vision with the balance of full story telling. As a result, those who seek beauty in her work remain necessarily skeptical of melodramatic truth; and those Marxist/feminist seekers of truth, skeptical of or confused by the beauty.

As her technique progresses—always lyrical, and including a medley of viewpoints, sudden poetic commentary, authorial rhetoric, accuracy of dialogue and a voice—to the internalization of consciousness and unfolding of memory and image, to the whirr-blur of fragmentary consciousness of many characters in a single "action" in *Requa*—it demands as much attention from the reader just to puzzle out what's happening, as say an Elizabethan play (not in its outline, but its nuance). Oddly, for me, technique at this point dissipates sympathy.

MEMORIES OF HENRY BROMELL IN BOSTON

I met Henry Bromell through Tillie Olsen in 1973. He was already publishing stories in *The New Yorker*, and had been her student during her residency at Amherst College in 1970. Tillie was now in residence at MIT. I had written her from *Ploughshares*, praising *Tell Me A Riddle*, sharing the latest issues of *Ploughshares*, and asking for new work. Tillie and I also had her publisher, Sam Lawrence, in common, whom I knew through Richard Yates and through my research on Brian Moore. In any case, Tillie alerted to me to Bromell, and also to Scott Turow and Fred Pfeil, also from Amherst. Bromell's stories, soon to be collected in *The Slightest Distance* (1974) and published by Houghton Mifflin as winner of their discovery award, reminded me of F. Scott Fitzgerald in their wit, nostalgia, and focus on a patrician, State Department family, and on Scobie, the writerly son.

That year I was editing a special "realism" issue of *Ploughshares*, affirming varieties of realism in the face of critical pronouncements about its obsolescence. Turow wrote a review of Olsen's *Yonnandio* for the issue. He also recommended a story by Fred Pfeil, which I included.

Earlier, Sam Lawrence had put me in touch with Tim O'Brien, and Tim had sent me a chapter of his first novel, "A Man of Melancholy Disposition," which I included, and when Tim moved to Cambridge to become a Neiman fellow, I asked him to co-edit another fiction issue with Bromell and me. This appeared in 1976. Bromell included a story by a friend, Meredith Steinbach, whom he'd met at Iowa, where he had been teaching. He also solicited a story from Mary Lavin, "A House to Let," and wrote an admiring profile of her for his contribution (a connection that later led to her reading for *Ploughshares* at a Cambridge fundraiser). "Her people feel more than they think," Bromell wrote. "She builds these characters from gesture, mannerism, speech, dream, work, with a language that is rich, suggestive, and lyrical."

O'Brien, on the other hand, asked Seymour Epstein for an address about realism that Epstein had delivered at Breadloaf, and solicited a story from John Irving, whom he'd also met there. His own contribution was "Going After Cacciato," which subsequently won the Best American Short Story, O'Henry, and Pushcart awards, and served as the opening chapter of his 1978 novel of the same name, winner of the National Book Award.

Bromell's younger brother, Nick, was also a writer, though more scholar, critic, and journalist than Henry.[*] Nick had graduated from Amherst as well, and was editing the *Boston Review*. I don't recall whether Henry ever wrote for them, but Henry remained in Boston until the publication of his second collection of stories, *I Know Your Heart, Marco Polo*, which appeared in 1979. He invited me for drinks and dinner once to a Boston apartment he shared with a stylish career woman, who wasn't

---

[*] http://www.umass.edu/english/faculty/Bromell.html

a writer, but who might have been a photographer or graphic designer. They seemed confident, admiring, and happy with each other. I remember stiff martinis, Henry slouching on a futon as we chatted, and my sense of being presented to the woman as the mendicant amusement. Shortly afterwards, Henry left for Hollywood. I continued sending him *Ploughshares* there, and hoped he'd keep in touch as an advisory editor, forward any writers he found to us, and perhaps send us work of his own. (Two or three years later, the girlfriend called me asking if I remembered her and had any news of Henry.)

Years passed. Then I discovered his name among the credits for one of my favorite TV shows, *Northern Exposure* (1990-95). He was listed as story editor, and then as writer for several episodes himself. In the spring of 2001, he sent me a note at *Ploughshares* to say that he had a new novel coming out from Knopf, *Little America*. He was having a book party at his parents' house in Cambridge, and it would be good to see me. If Bromell had "gone Hollywood," I thought, and had sold out fiction writing for TV, then *Little America* proved that the writer had not only survived, but grown, and was making a comeback. He had married and had a son. Always a slender, handsome guy, he now looked more grizzled. His father, tall and white-haired and wearing a suit, seemed elegantly at one with guests I recognized as retired Harvard faculty, including my first woman teacher, Anne Ferry, and her husband, David Ferry, the poet and Wordsworth scholar, both of whom had Amherst connections through Reuben Brower. The house had antiques, book cases, and dark paneling, and on the dinner table, over which there hung a chandelier, a stack of Henry's novel, which was for sale and for signing, following on a brief reading. My own first novel, *The Marriage Of Anna Maye Potts*, had just been published by

combined with humor and intensity, and all while writing and producing with an intergrity that joined literature to popular TV and film. At this juncture, I am sorry, given the focus at Emerson College (where I have made a teaching career) that we never invited him for an honorary degree.

I noticed that the VP of Showtime, Bromell's boss, was also an Amherst graduate.

HB's film *Panic* (on Netflix) deserves the status of *Fargo* as a cult classic. The mode is psychoanalytic satire: first, of the cutthroat (literally) family business of killing for pay that underpins normality and the good life; second, of the parental brainwashing of sons and grandsons, and of the delicious, sly contest between shrink and father for the good son's soul. Casting is fantastic, with William Macy, Tracy Ullman, and Neve Campbell. Style, wit and conception recall *Northern Exposure,* but the connection of family bonds and violent crime suggests *Brotherhood* and—with Uncle Sam as father—*Rubicon* and *Homeland* to come.

REMEMBERING JAMES ALAN MCPHERSON

I first met Jim McPherson when he was twenty-five to my twenty-six and finishing his law degree at Harvard. A mutual friend introduced us because I had just returned to my Harvard PhD program from the Iowa Writers' Workshop and Jim was considering taking an MFA there. I'd read none of Jim's work and had no idea that he'd published in the *Atlantic*, had studied with Alan Lebowitz, had been mentored by Edward Weeks, and was finishing his first collection, *Hue and Cry*. I described my Iowa experience to him: that I'd begun a novel, encouraged by Richard Yates, and then when Yates left to write a Hollywood script, had been discouraged enough by Nelson Algren, his replacement, that I suffered writer's block. Except for Yates, I'd felt marooned. Jim thanked me, but went anyway, and worked briefly with Yates, who, according to Blake Bailey's Yates biography, told him: "'They're rushing you. Slow down.' and started to tease through McPherson's paragraphs, pointing out all the little things that need to be 'fixed' prior to publication."

In the next few years, I finished my PhD; couldn't find work; met my wife, Connie; and began *Ploughshares* with

Peter O'Malley and some local writers (including a few Iowa alums) who frequented the Plough and Stars pub in Cambridge. I kept following Jim's work, especially his *Atlantic* cover interview with Ralph Ellison (which inspired my own *Ploughshares* interview with Yates), his journalism about the Blackstone Rangers, and *Hue and Cry.* I wrote him a fan letter, c/o the *Atlantic,* in 1973 and asked him for a story for the special realism issue I was editing. He asked his agent to return unpublished stories to him and promised to send "the better of the two" along. He hand-delivered the hilarious "I Am an American." He had typed the manuscript on his flight east from San Francisco, and after it appeared in *Ploughshares* in 1974, he asked for the manuscript back, but it had been thrown out by our typesetter, which annoyed him.

I like to think that he was deliberately turning to our literary magazine as a cause, having been disillusioned, as Allen Gee relates in "Old School," the longform essay published as a *Ploughshares Solo* last fall, by the *Atlantic*'s publishing an article that argued that heredity rather than environment limited black intelligence—an article he had strenuously opposed as a contributing editor.

Our first real collaboration came many years later, when we coedited a fiction-only issue of *Ploughshares* in 1985. Jim was teaching at Iowa by then, having left the University of Virginia, where he'd felt that he was both window dressing and a target of envy. *Elbow Room* had been published in 1977 and had been out of print when it won the Pulitzer Prize for Fiction in 1978. He'd been one of the first MacArthur Genius Grant fellows in 1981. But then he'd undergone a bitter divorce and lost custody of his young daughter, thanks to what he later described as the racist establishment in Virginia, and the invitation to teach at Iowa had been a blessing.

As we approached sorting through submissions, what

mattered to us both—in what seemed a confused and hostile literary climate—were the stories themselves. Mostly, our visions overlapped. Jim championed work that questioned cultural clichés and that chafed against closed mindsets, especially those concerning "style." He sought and favored stories, as he wrote in the *Washington Post*, that reflected America's "diversity, touch[ed] a variety of its people, laugh[ed] at its craziness, distill[ed] wisdom from its tragedies, and attempt[ed] to synthesize all this ... without going crazy."

We collaborated, again, on the 1990 double issue of *Ploughshares*. Following the magazine's tradition of themed issues, Jim had proposed selecting work related to the notion of "confronting difference," with models such as Stephen Crane's "The Monster" or Sherwood Anderson's "Hands," but then Don Lee, as managing editor, suggested narrowing the difference to race and joined in the collaboration. In the editing, we rejected submissions where the inclusion of characters of color seemed arbitrary, and where writing perpetuated racial clichés. We were looking for awareness, sensitivity, and responsibility.

The 1998 collection *Fathering Daughters: Reflections by Men* was our next collaboration, this time with Helene Atwan of Beacon Press, in which we solicited original essays from a range of prominent writer-fathers about their bonds with their daughters. Jim contributed his own essay, "Disneyland," where he described his efforts to sustain a close relationship with his daughter, Rachel, in her growing up, despite his limited visitation rights. Where the father-daughter bond was culturally under strain at the time, we hoped the essays we gathered filled a certain void and encouraged ongoing conversation and healing.

Jim guest-edited his last fiction issue of *Ploughshares*

for the fall issue of 2008. I had returned as interim editor-in-chief, following Don Lee's twelve-year tenure as my successor. Jim had published *Crabcakes* (1998) and *A Region Not Home* (2000), but at this point, serious health issues had begun to trouble him. Still, he rose to our occasion. In his introduction, he mentioned "neighboring": "If there is a common thread in the stories here, I think it must be the communal effort to gain perspective on the highly complex areas of our fuzzy and fragmented American reality." He saw hope in the candidacy of Obama as an omni-American. "One source of his appeal is that he thinks and operates beyond race and class and sexual orientation—beyond all the social categories that function as substitutes for a transcendent American identity." This, of course, described Jim's own agenda.

ON FACT AND FICTION

In the late 1960s, I believed in pure fiction, and as a writer set out to imagine and portray the inner life of working-class characters in my father's candy factory. I also kept a writer's notebook on the side, where I vented and mulled about my escapades and follies as a lonely graduate student. In an entire chapter of my novel—"Ballgame" (1971)—I transferred my first-person notebook description of attending a Redsox vs. Twins pennant game into the third person of my old maid character, Anna Maye Potts. What came alive in the fiction was a kind of agoraphobic panic, causing my former mentor Richard Yates to praise: "Don't change a word."

Other times, the novel painted me into corners. The widowed and womanizing foreman character, Louie, who would later marry Anna Maye, struggled alone to care for his mentally disabled daughter. This was a life-fact I had heard about an actual foreman in my father's factory, but lacking any experience with down syndrome, I volunteered at a nearby state school in order to learn, feel, and imagine the circumstances more accurately. The novel took years to complete and then more years to publish.

During its writing, I married, had children, and struggled to find work, while also struggling to found a literary magazine, support my family, and deal with the deaths of my parents.

When I interviewed Richard Yates (with Geoffrey Clark) in 1972 and asked about autobiographical fiction, Yates responded first about *Revolutionary Road*: "There's plenty of myself in that book—every character in the book was partially based on myself, or on some aspect of myself, or on people I knew or composites of people I knew, but each of them was very carefully put through a kind of fictional prism, so that in the finished book, I like to think the reader can't really find the author anywhere." Then about his "autobiographical blowout," the story, "Builders": "I think that story did work, because it was formed. It was objectified. Somehow, and maybe it was just luck, I managed to avoid both of the two terrible traps that lie in the path of autobiographical fiction—self-pity and self-aggrandizement....Anybody can scribble out a confession or a memoir or a diary or a chronicle of personal experience, but how many writers can *form* that kind of material?"

I loved Tim O'Brien's distinction in *The Things They Carried* between happening truth and story truth. To tell a true war story (or any story), you need to avoid the conventional lies of heroism and valor and instead expose the obscenity and absurdity of combat. Also: "Absolute occurrence is irrelevant. A thing may happen and be a total lie; another thing may not happen and be truer than the truth."

I abandoned fiction and turned to writing my family's story as I had heard and witnessed it. I felt that the felt truth of my supposedly privileged background was too important to put through "a kind of fictional prism." I also experimented with personal essays.

One of these is "Bungee." I was fascinated by watching bungee jumpers on the cliffside tower at High Camp at the Squaw Valley Writers Conference. Kids, tourists, thrill seekers: would I do that? Would I take the risk? Back home in Boston, I described my own jump in detail, when in fact, I had only watched. I ended my account on a Tim O'Brien-ish note: "Did I jump or didn't I? Who cares?" I read it at Squaw Valley the next year, with everybody convinced that I had jumped; so at that point I decided to try, paid my money, climbed the scaffold and did—literally—jump. All I learned from the happening fact was that the fall felt faster than I had imagined, with no time to think. Otherwise, I had imagined everything correctly. My point was that most experiences were like that, imaginable. That we don't have to bullfight to write believably about bullfighting, or love, or crime, or suicide. We can have the experience in imagination without the consequence in life. As Eudora Welty put it, "A sheltered life can be a daring life as well. For all serious daring starts from within."

In other stories, I evolved a narrative persona. Late middle age, a father concerned with raising a daughter and son in a rapidly changing culture. Then a grandfather. A bookish husband with a brave-hearted, loving wife. However, in using family material, I also risked offending those I loved for the sake of my own truths. I invaded privacies. My wife objected. I thought my sister understood and didn't object, but then she did, and I had to live with the pain of having caused them both pain for the sake of the art. Lowell's confessional poetry was one inspiration ("Yet why not say what happened? / Pray for the grace of accuracy"), but then I also read more widely in memoir, admiring Frank Conroy (who insisted that *Stop Time* was a novel), Tobias Wolff, Mary Karr, and others.

There had to be detachment and a distance from myself. In my full-length memoir, *Sweet Dreams,* the distance came from time. In my mid-sixties, I set my narrating self in my mid-fifties, and from that vantage told my childhood, adolescence, and young adulthood. After writing "objective" fiction, I found it freeing to write in first-person, and in a voice and vocabulary closer to my own, while also foregrounding subjectivity as part of the art.

Though Norman Mailer called himself Mailer in his nonfiction books, I resisted pretending to third person objectivity by calling myself by name. I liked the drama of struggling for perspective. I liked involving the reader in issues of self-reliability. On the other hand, having written a first-person account of getting a therapeutic massage and reliving core emotions through body memory, when I did publish it, I changed all the "I's" to a third person last name, Harris, the thinnest of disguises, but one that helped my wife to accept my writing about our marriage.

My former student and successor at *Ploughshares*, Don Lee, mocked literary Boston and the magazine itself in his novel *The Collective* (Norton, 2012). His narrator, Eric, takes an MFA at "Walden" rather than Emerson College, where he interns at *Palaver* rather than *Ploughshares*, and describes the editor as "my principle workshop teacher [which I was], Evan Pavirono, a British-Italian scholar, bon vivant, and wastrel. He was a charismatic, towering presence at six-foot-five, beefy verging on portly, with thick brown hair he kept long and swept back," which describes the co-founder of *Ploughshares*, Peter O'Malley, rather than me. In fact, I have been erased and replaced by my opposite. Should I feel offended? Unsure of Lee's intention, I let it pass.

And one last twist on this subject. Having known

Yates as a person and writer for years, and having read all of his fiction closely, I knew firsthand about his psychotic breakdowns, and worried about his losing generosity of perspective in his fictionalized self-portraits (think of the contrast between John Givings in *Revolutionary Road* and the "poet" Wilder in *Disturbing the Peace*). But only after reading Blake Bailey's detailed biography of Yates after his death, did I appreciate how obsessively autobiographical all of his fiction was, and how hard he had struggled to be one on whom nothing was lost.

WHAT IF?

Here I am, running, sixty-five, shorts and t-shirt, beautiful fall day, one of my rare runs anymore outside of the gym. I have run down two blocks from my house, crossed the bridge over the Charles River, then headed right and down the new bike path through woods along the river, the yellow, orange, red, and green leaves closing the sky, all glowing with sunlight, the river visible through gaps in the bushes and trees, with maybe some scattered geese swimming. I pass people walking, older people mostly, some with dogs. From behind I hear bikes coming, and make room, and a man and a woman sweep past. But mostly I'm alone, and after three or five minutes of jogging, trying to keep my eyes up, as if a balloon were lifting my chest (for form), I need to slow to a walk, enjoying the scenery, then start up jogging again. In all, the wood path goes one mile, crosses the river again on a walking bridge, continues close to the river and shielded by foliage and landscaping from industrial buildings, then ends up a hill behind the Stop and Shop supermarket and emerges onto a busy road. Left, over another bridge, and across the street, the path continues towards Waltham for another two or three miles. I don't want to go that far. I could turn around and retrace the path, enjoying it again from a new direction, heading home. But I decide to turn right, jogging down the sidewalk and then up to lights at the busy intersection with Pleasant Street, where I cross and follow the sidewalk for half a mile along Seyon Street past the dreary, low industrial buildings on both sides that have been abandoned by Raytheon and only partially re-tenanted. Walking again, I cross over the intersection at Seyon and Waltham Street and turn right, quickening to a jog along the sidewalk that borders the Gore Estate, its waist-high stone wall and densely planted woods to my left. Thirty yards ahead I see a woman pushing a baby carriage towards me. We are strangers. Me the senior citizen and grandfather, enjoying the day, enjoying my vitality and sweaty in mid-jog, her the young mother (I can see she is young, my daughter's age or younger, smiling and proud). Distance closes. I know to watch my step. I remember there is a metal stub somewhere ahead in the sidewalk, perhaps four inches high, where a sign-post has been removed. The sidewalk is narrow, but there should be room enough to pass the carriage without stepping into the street. I am preoccupied with my run, strong again. Drawing closer, I mean to smile, to bless the baby as I pass, and she pushes the carriage as close to the wall as she can, when suddenly I've tripped and everything slows down. I've fallen before on runs, tripping over dog leashes or roots, and tried to break the fall by rolling on my shoulder. I've opened gashes and bruised shins. My choice is either to twist away and spill hard onto the edge of the curb and into the street, the way of serious injury; or, in mid-fall, to lurch the other way, and crash into the carriage. I twist toward the carriage. I am crashing full weight into the carriage and in some awful, irreversible way, into the baby. But the mother halts in time and somehow I manage to recover balance, only partially jarring and folding myself over the front of the carriage, as my left hand catches and braces against the wall. I stand back, flushed, and apologize, heart pounding. She asks am I all right? I'm fine, I say, thank you. The baby is undisturbed, as she fusses and hovers over it. I nod, smile, and step past them, starting to jog again, as if nothing's happened. But we both know something could have happened. That despite the beauty of the day, despite beneficence and pride of being, out of nowhere, in a blink: the unthinkable was possible. Carriage crushed, baby, and all. 911. Lives could have been changed forever.

REPLAYING DOOM

I've played and replayed *Doom 2*, the classic first-person-shooter game, for some thirty years so far with pleasure, frustration, triumph and satisfaction; although also with some guilt. However gripping, it is a largely vapid pastime, requiring skill more than talent, and leaves behind no artifact or wisdom. Or so I've thought. If poetry, according to Sir Philip Sydney, is that which "keeps old men from the chimney corner and children from their play," my hours of playing the *Doom* series have kept me away from literature, family, work and friends.

Doom 3D was released in 1993 and *Doom 2* a year later by ID Games, while both its creators, Johns Romero and Carmack, were still twenty-somethings. According to David Gusher's *Masters of Doom: How Two Guys Created an Empire and Transformed Pop Culture* (Random, 2003), both had come from broken families, and had graduated from arcade gaming to school computer labs before becoming hackers. They first collaborated on *Wolfenstein 3D*, which helped to popularize first-person-shooter games, but *Doom 3D* set a new standard for video gaming in general. It combines concepts and graphics from such sci-fi films as *Alien*, soundtracks of heavy-metal rock, and situations and player choices similar to those of the role-playing board game, *Dungeons and Dragons*; but as Carmack puts it, "Story in a game is like story in a porn movie; it's expected to be there, but it's not that important."

If you've never played *Doom* and its sequels, here is a brief description (if you have, please skip). On a PC, with your mouse and keyboard keys for control, you take the perspective of a single Space Marine on screen as he aims a pistol ahead and fires when you hit the shoot command. Your mission is to evade or defeat a demonic horde from Hell (and/or another universe) by sabotaging their extra-terrestrial bases and strongholds. You don't know your way initially and as you advance to explore caves, tunnels, castles, corridors, factories and craggy landscapes, you battle a hierarchy of clever, but non-human monsters, ranging from ape-like imps that throw fireballs, to fanged attack dogs, to bee-like lost souls, to flying tomato-like creatures that spit explosives, to over-sized barons with blasters, to spider-brains, to giant and all-but-indestructible bosses firing missiles. You can turn, crouch, jump, walk, run; shoot and destroy—as long as your health and ammo last. If wounded you can find health boosts, but if health declines to zero, you have to start the game over. As you progress, you also pick up more powerful weapons, ammo, armor, and other supplies. The carnage is realistic and graphic. Demons remain splattered as roadkill, sometimes in heaps. There are howls, cries, growls, and groans, along with explosions and driving music. You are immersed in 3D action and space, evoked by 2D means. The fight/flight thrill is sustained as you work your way through the map and traps, locate three keys, and then the final switch that allows you to exit to the next of, yes, 32 levels. Other features include a save command (allowing you a do-over with foreknowledge at any point) and cheat codes that allow you to be invincible, pass through walls, and wield a plasma blaster with unlimited ammo, the ultimate weapon.

No previous computer game had been this brutal, fast, and visceral, created 3D views, Mannerist habitats, fun-house surprises, and complex tests of persistence and wit; and despite advances in hardware since (including innovations in AI, AR, and VR), none has surpassed it. Custom fails to stale its variety; and its spell remains potent.

But still I wonder whether addictive play is innocent or dangerous. If escapist, is it as destructive as drugs, gambling, or sex (*Doom* has been called a "cyberopioid" and "heroinware")? Or is it beneficial in any way, like running?

❧❧❧ ❧❧❧ ❧❧❧

Even before the release of *Doom 3D*, moral guardians blamed graphic violence in film, video, and video games for corrupting youth, but almost at once Senator Joseph Lieberman and other lawmakers singled out *Doom* as a contributing factor in the school shooting at Columbine in 1996 (and in the others that followed). Both the adolescent killers at Columbine had been devotees of *Doom* and one had boasted to his journal that the massacre would be "like playing *Doom*," and that his shotgun "was right out of *Doom*." (Although it has never been found, he may also have modified a level of *Doom* to resemble his school's layout, and its demons to resemble classmates and teachers.) Watch-dog attempts to ban video games eventually failed, yet did persuade industry leaders to self-regulate by posting adults-only ratings. In 2010, critic David Grossman cited *Doom* in particular as "a mass murder simulator," and reported that the U.S. Army even used it (and other FPS games) for combat training.

※ ※ ※

And what of *Hamlet*, or even worse, *Titus Andronicus*—no matter how ironic the morals, monstrous the figures, or cartoonish the gore? And aren't *Doom*'s targets *demons*, after all; and the heroic shooter's mission, to save humanity? Games don't kill people, people do, insist game designers and *Doom* fans. Meanwhile, so-called ludologists have attempted to link FPS games to the higher arts.

One game designer and scholar argues that "The same impulse towards play that drives our behavior in playing a first person shooter is present where we read a line from Homer or look at cave paintings" (Bryan Upton, *The Aesthetics of Play*, 2015). He proposes a "heuristics of play as a critical tool for understanding how art in general goes about structuring experience," and offers such key terms as "active constraints" (rules, with give and take between player and system), opportunities for meaningful action, "states" (an evolving record of how a player moves within the system), flow, threat zones, phase space, horizon of intent, strategy, consequence, and satisfaction. "Day to day life," he writes, "presents an unfolding sequence of choices, but these choices aren't shaped by a coherent systems of rules," whereas a video game presents us "with an evolving state that implies the underlying nature of the rules, but the rules themselves remain hidden." Games supposedly "help us to understand understanding" and "generate the experience of self."

Playing *Doom*, he implies, is like reading a poem or novel. "The path we take to get [meaning] is "convoluted and indirect...because navigating a well-constructed system of constraints is interesting and fun."

Ralph Koster in *A Theory of Fun for Game Design* (2005), exhorts us "Go play! In poetry and prose, play in wit, play in form, play in association, illogic, metaphor, allusions." For him, play exercises the brain. Fun translates into "mentally mastering problems...and problems can be aesthetic, physical, or social." He particularly praises flow, or "learning in a context where there is no pressure."

Such efforts sound defensive and pretentious. And yet. Video games may have replaced narrative film as the "art" medium of our wired age. Koster argues that "entertainment becomes art when the communicative element is either novel or exceptionally well done."

Another brilliant feature of *Doom 2* was the free availability of its code, so that amateur hackers could modify it. This resulted in thousands of MODS becoming downloadable online as long as players owned a licensed copy of the ID original. The maps for each level could be changed creatively, as could the weapons, background graphics, hero and monsters. Otherwise, the rules and play remained the same. Many of the MODS became experiences special enough to keep replaying. Some were camp parodies, where the Marine became Batman or .007 or the Cyber Boss became Barney the Dinosaur. Some are more elaborate than the ID original. Their novelty seems limitless.

Over time, I've experienced "gamer nostalgia." Returning to a familiar map is like returning to my hometown and knowing the streets, topography, routes, and turns. I'd been here before. I half-remember this secret or that, this short-cut, this strategy or that. Earlier lessons I had learned.

❦ ❦ ❦

For better or worse, gaming has become a staple for post-millennial generations. In a recent interview Carmack, forty-nine and the CTO of Oculus, the VR headset company (he has since stepped down to concentrate on AI), described "E-sports and competitive gaming" as a world-wide phenomenon, complete with professional players. The dawn of this was with *Doom*. "When I did the *Quake* Tournament, I gave my first Ferrari as first prize (won by Thresh [a gaming superstar]). Only a year later, there was another tournament with a $100M prize." His interviewer adds: "And today you've got the amazing celebrity of the top pro players. They're now legitimate sports stars...Top earners like Tiger Woods are out-earned by three times, three million. The Super Bowl in South Korea for gaming dwarfs that for the football in the U.S. Millions are tuning in."

However, attempts to make feature films out of *Doom* have flopped, lacking any viewer interaction; while attempts to turn popular films into role-playing FPS games, where the player is James Bond, say, have enjoyed some passing success.

Notes Jay David Bolter in *Wired*: "New audiences... seek their cultural centers elsewhere—in video games and social media. One of the principal pleasures offered by both video games and social media is the experience of flow." We're swept along. Point by point choices and actions blur in motion, like flip cards, or cells of movie film, or fragments into meaning. We discover grace, like a pro full-back evading tacklers with twists, plunges, dodgings, straight-arms, and speed, until crossing the goal line, ecstatic and triumphing; from inertia into glory.

※ ※ ※

Jane McGonigal, a "game evangelist," believes that "intense concentration in a game can be harnessed for social change by turning real-world problems into collective online games." A dubious prospect, I think. But so is the familiar claim that poetry (or narrative itself) improves mutual understanding and our capacity to feel, despite the equally familiar objection that high culture and Wagner didn't keep the Nazis from being Nazis. I simply can't imagine a version of *Doom* where the demons learn through "play" to be humane. Or where "humans" learn not only to out-think, evade, and outgun challenging demons, but manage to transform them and to be transformed.

Perhaps *Doom* engrosses precisely because I am exasperated with "real-world problems," which seem unsolvable. It's a relief to take action as the righteous, persistent and resourceful Marine. And if I've only played at the medium level, or if I've used save and replay for second chances, if sometimes I've been stymied and had to resort to cheat codes; still better players than I am exist and have won fairly—look at the Youtube recordings of best games.

I love the programmers' joke hidden in the impossible level 32 of *Doom 2*. If you use God-mode and clipping (which allows you to pass through walls), you can penetrate the hole in the forehead of a sphinx-sized supreme demon, from which flying cubes steadily issue—cubes that land and turn into endless ranks of demons—and there you find a living and tormented human head on a stake—recognizable as John Romano's. Bombard that and you win.

⁂ ⁂ ⁂

I think of Shakespeare's Prospero as the ultimate designer, who puts his enemies through a dream of shipwreck and survival on the strange island where they marooned him years before with his young daughter. Now under his spell they are tormented and act out their viciousness on each other, until Prospero's hench-spirit, Ariel (portrayed as a robot in one sci-fi film adaptation), reminds him to see them as fellow humans.

"The rarer action is / In virtue than in vengeance," Prospero decides, then breaks his spell and forgives the repentants as he wishes to be forgiven, though the problem of Caliban, the island's native and the offspring of a witch, remains. Indeed, most recently, post-colonial, feminist, Marxist, and anti-racist readers have sympathized with Caliban and condemned the Eurocentric, patriarchal Prospero, who may abjure magic at last, but is still more at fault than he admits. And there's the rub: what can we do, this side of Utopia, to transcend division, violence and crime? In life, it seems we only have imperfect attempts, ranging from the well-intentioned to the self-hating and sadistic. We don't have innocent solutions. How do we prevent recurrences? How do we rehabilitate the Nazis after World War 2? How do we reason with fanatics? Saint Genet? Jihady John? Klansmen and supremacists? And what about psychopaths? Where imagination fails, our games at least keep teasing our philosophy.

METADOODLE

I doodled mostly military motifs as a school boy: tanks, cannons, guns, bombers in the margins or covers of my notebooks, sometimes a horse, or my girl-friend's name or even my own name, along with the usual curlicues and crosshatches: no deep message or design. Fifty years later, however, I sit in my academic department meeting beside Murray Schwartz, a psychoanalytic critic, and assume he is as bored as I am, since he doodles on the agenda handout. But he raises his hand suddenly and adds an important point. Another colleague knits while she listens. They both claim that these absent-minded side activities help them to focus. And Murray's designs, as yet another colleague raves, are so elegant and inventive that they deserve to be saved. He becomes famous for them among us.

Neither drawings nor sketches, true doodles are "deep thinking in disguise," according to Sunni Brown, author of *The Doodle Revolution* (Portfolio, 2014). I don't draw idly, and I don't think visually, but I do doodle in prose, which I distinguish from free, rough draft, or automatic writing. I aspire to Feste's "corrupting" of words, especially since in such dallying begins responsibility: "A sentence is but a cheverel glove to a good wit, how quickly the wrong side may be turned outward." Take any fashionable word, motif, or idea, one we use without thinking, even the word "doodle" itself. What does it mean in such familiar contexts as "Yankee doodle dandy" (an idler? a buffoon? a resourceful revolutionary? an upstart?). What usage comes to mind, especially to *my* mind as a person and as a writer and reader (a cheese doodle, for instance:, all taste and air, squiggly in shape)? What do I know, or think I know, or don't know I knew? What can I learn? What examples rise from memory and from literature, philosophy, and art? What special meanings do the dictionary, thesaurus, and Wikipedia suggest (e.g."The term Doodle first appeared in English in the early seventeenth century and is thought to be derived from the Low German [a language close to Dutch] dudel, meaning "playing music badly" or Dödel, meaning "fool" or "simpleton")? Where do synonyms (e.g. "fiddle, tinker, monkey, putter, mess, goof, trifle around") and antonyms (e.g. the opposite of the doodle dandy would be a formal, British general or aristocrat) lead? I try to earn some expert status, out-associating, -questioning, -and -imagining the reader.

To "think in disguise" is to lower the defenses of reason, much as dreaming does. Narrative logic, exposition, and rational argumentation no longer apply. Form is free. Association, at best, is unforeseen and gymnastic. Suggestion itself is meaning. Perhaps that is why psychoanalysts ask patients both to to free associate on words and to see designs in ink blots. Apparent nonsense provokes imagination. "Very like a whale, my lord." Yet there are still rules. "Though this be madness, yet there is method in't. How pregnant sometimes his replies are. A happiness that often madness hits on, which reason and sanity could not so prosperously be delivered of."

The DNA of words fascinates me. As does their use in pop and vernacular culture; and often their dimensions in Shakespeare, whose plays are part of my life's thinking, and who loads familiar words with multifaceted contexts and meanings ("nothing will come of nothing.... I see feelingly....Look there, look there!"). I love animation's art of morphing, or transforming, as well; one shape blooming into another, a bird into a plane or plane into a crucifix, shape shifting. In dwelling on a given subject, I move from paragraph to paragraph, phrase to phrase, idea to idea, improvising and riffing like jazz, or assembling fragments like collage, where meanings from different contexts combine to make new sense. My stream of consciousness meanders, but still follows gravity.

The figure that a prose doodle makes is similar to poetry's, as Robert Frost describes the process: "it inclines to the impulse, it assumes direction with the first line laid down, it runs a course of lucky events, and ends in a clarification of life." Or as Wallace Stevens puts it: "The poem of the mind in the act of finding / What will suffice."

The genre John D'Agata calls "the lyric essay"* sounds like a doodle by any other name. "It might move by association, leaping from one path of thought to another by way of imagery or connotation, advancing by juxtaposition or sidewinding poetic logic. Generally it is short, concise and punchy like a prose poem. But it may meander, making use of other genres when they serve its purpose: recombinant, it samples the techniques of fiction, drama, journalism, song, and film....[It] often

---

* http://www.hws.edu/academics/senecareview/lyricessay.aspx

accretes by fragments, taking shape mosaically—its import visible only when one stands back and sees it whole. The stories it tells may be no more than metaphors. Or, story-less, it may spiral in on itself, circling the core of a single image or idea, without climax, without a paraphrasable theme."

For the individual doodler, each word has its own valence; some feel highly charged, others don't. *War*, say; or *Peace;* among other standard subjects of aphorisms and proverbs (such as Francis Bacon's, William Blake's, or Nietzsche's). See what comes to mind. What words need rescue from neglect, overuse, or disrepute? Do we use them without thinking or even to stop thinking, as with "*War is Peace*"? What words seem so obvious that they lead nowhere? How do you tell a true war story? asks Tim O'Brien. And Falstaff, of course, catechizes that word *honor* as mere "air," thereby discounting all the words we live and die for—except the word *life* itself.

So far, one word, "magic"—a recommendation from my granddaughters, who love Merlin, Harry Potter, Gandalf and My Little Pony on TV—has failed to inspire me, although I suspect that it is on the secular mind for serious reasons, including our reliance on technologies and powers that are beyond everyday understanding. As usual, Shakespeare has suggestions to contribute, along with Ingmar Bergman, "That Old Black Magic That You So Well," Garcia Marquez and the Magical Realists, not to mention Harry Houdini or David Copperfield.

Each doodle is an expedition. The most rewarding lead into wonder, into fields of meaning and the mysteries of metaphor. Some carry the promise of collective wisdom. Some demand fancy and imagination. Some invoke new research and discoveries. Some reveal outmoded agendas and biases, or promote new ones. As George Orwell warns, language is "an instrument we shape for our own purposes," and our purposes can be generous and well-meaning as well as tyrannous. In any case, the literary doodle—give or take the thinker's ironies—dramatizes how rather than what to think. And for me, for now, it feels more liberating than other forms. It absorbs me. It takes effort, labor and resourcefulness as well as inspiration. It evolves its own particular rhythm and music. And each time, who knows where the writer and reader will come out?

DAYENU

Neither my daughter, Ruth, nor my son, Dave, ever knew grandfathers. Connie's divorced father died shortly after I met her. My father died after we had been married, but before Connie's pregnancy with Ruth. I did take Dave as an adolescent to Colorado to meet my brother Jack, who was his uncle, but who at twelve years my senior had been like a father to me. Ruth had known Jack too, somewhat. He had visited us in Watertown and read books to her as a child, then taken her up with us in his 1939 Staggerwing, which he had flown to Hanscom Field. Later he visited us in Iowa City where I was teaching one summer, and Connie and both kids had driven out to join me in my mother's old Buick. However, having grown up with friends who had real, living grandfathers, Ruth wanted her own children to know me, us.

Ruth gave birth to Eva in Cartegena, Colombia, as a single Mom. The father, Khari, a hip-hop performer and kick-boxer, was a deadbeat. Ruth had left the relationship and taken a Fulbright to Colombia; then had learned that she was pregnant. Connie went down for the birth. Ruth and the baby returned to Boston and lived with us, before trying to live again with Khari. When Khari couldn't pay rent, Ruth first moved to her own apartment, then took Eva back to Cartegena, where they lived in an artists' hotel. She met Diego as a tenant there. He made jewelry and studied history at the university.

In Boston, Eva had fixated on me. With Ruth, I walked her in her stroller along the Charles River path, one of my running haunts. Eva and I cuddled and watched TV, especially the *Berington Bears Show*, where Eva studied the father bear and his difference from Poppa Khari, who only made occasional, glad-handing visits to our house and took her for trial overnights. I sometimes called her Ruth by mistake. I read books with her and watched her grow. Now she chose Diego for her father and conspired with him to propose to her Mom. Connie, David and I went down for the wedding, along with some Boston friends and Connie's brother. Eva was the flower girl.

Soon Ruth was pregnant again. She and Diego had rented a house, which we helped them later to buy. Maya was born, and after visiting to help, Connie brought back pictures of her. On my Spring vacation, while Connie worked, and Dave was finishing his MA, I made the trip alone to meet the baby (now almost four months) and to bless their settled life. Ruth taught English and Diego made designer lamps from gourds, to be sold in the States. I slept on an air-mattress in Eva's room. Diego was welcoming, although we could only communicate in gestures, since I lacked Spanish and he English. They had their routine. Holding Maya's 4-month-old, fresh gaze, I thought of cycles. Eva was a school girl now, wearing her uniform for second grade and helping to care for her sister. "Which do you like better, Boston or Cartegena?" she asked. I liked them both, I said, but Boston was best for me because it was my life and work and language; but she was lucky to have two worlds where most people only have one.

Ruth and Diego both believed in social justice and in hip hop as a medium for change, especially as it voiced impoverished youth. They had begun collaborating on Diego's lamps, with Ruth sketching out designs on the shell of each gourd, which Diego then drilled, and Ruth next painted in bright colors. When furnished with an interior socket and bulb, the lamp cast designs of light and shadow on the ceiling and walls. Diego took videos of Ruth's performing her lyrics as well and posted them to Youtube. Diego's workspace was in a corner of the kitchen, where he kept a computer, speakers, and his tools. They struggled for private time and sometimes worked late at night. They shared friends, and welcomed guests. They had a paying boarder in a room upstairs.

❧ ❧ ❧

They made their first trip to Boston in summer 2010. They took our downstairs bedroom with Maya (formerly Dave's room). And Eva took the second bedroom upstairs (formerly Ruth's). Connie and I loved filling our small house again. Dave had moved to an apartment in New York as he began internships and job searches. The next summer, while renting out the Cartegena house, Ruth's family visited again; and the next. Ruth earned certification to teach Kingian Nonviolence. She arranged exchanges between Colombian and stateside youth, performed herself, applied for grants, and worked to sell Diego's lamps and her paintings. In 2013, they planned to stay for six months, but the delay in Diego's Green Card application required them to stay longer. Connie and I worked full time teaching. Ruth had part-time teaching. Eva went to 3rd and 4th grade, with me driving her at 7am and waiting to pick her up at 2:30. Eva's friends came over. On my off days, I worked in my basement study, preparing classes and writing. Diego was marooned upstairs as Maya's primary caretaker. Taking breaks from my work, I tried to help by playing with her while he showered or cooked their meals. We stepped around each other like choreographed dancers. But there were growing tensions as well. Ruth and he had arguments in Spanish and he left for walks alone to cool off. When he did find construction jobs, he needed to be driven to sites unreachable by bus around Boston. We watched the girls when Diego and Ruth had shows or needed to go out. We welcomed their friends. We provided and shared food. But we also expected deference to our own habits and help with the house. When Diego, and also Ruth, played music too loud, we asked them to lower the volume or put on earphones. We spoke up about discipline and parenting issues. Maya needed more interactive play, we thought, instead of being parked in front of cartoons. We tolerated Diego's work on his lamps, with his whining drill or cans of toxic spray paint outside. We didn't like his marijuana smoke, which penetrated the house, even from outside. Predictably, he and Ruth sought an apartment of their own, which they couldn't yet afford.

In Spring 2014, on the recommendation of a friend of Connie's, Ruth was hired to teach Spanish by our Middle School, which offered health benefits and stable income. Diego got his green card at last and worked regularly for our neighbor, a landscaper. They found an affordable apartment down the street and Ruth commented on the irony, that after all these years of explorations and global adventures, here she was settled back in Watertown. We helped them lease a car. Our granddaughters were troubled to leave us, but they still see us for weekend overnights.

❧ ❧ ❧

How will Eva and Maya remember me? Maya probably won't remember much more than my withdrawal, like her father's, into adult privacy.

Of course, I am Grandee the fixer and assembler of toys and furniture. Grandee the grumbler. Grandee the recluse. Grandee the taxi, for errands. Grandee, the backup for Nana (and Nana the backup for Mom and Poppa). Grandee the battery supplier for toys and remotes. Grandee the band aid supplier. Grandee the go-to guy for electronics. Ball and bike-tire inflator; yard-man, grass cutter, snow shoveler. Grandee the runner and gym addict. Grandee the one-time swimmer and golfer. Grandee the man of habit, who eats at 11am and 5pm, despite the schedules of others, and lives on hot pockets and processed, microwave dinners. Grandee who isn't Jewish, but who stands quietly during Shabos prayers, then kisses foreheads in exchange. Grandee the cellar dweller, not to be disturbed, as he reads from stacks and shelves of grown up books, and as he types on his computer. Grandee, who clomps up his stairs periodi-cally, when summoned, or for emergencies. Grandee, who kills flies, and refuses to let anyone else use his swatter.

Maya and I seek common ground in play. Putting on the rug, for instance. Reading childrens' books. I draw cartoons for her, a dog, a giraffe, a duck, which she then imitates or colors in. At two or three she knew more Spanish than I did or do (Eva from an early age, as well, has translated for me and Diego when Ruth isn't around); in English, I try to correct her r's, which she pronounces as w's.

I am amused by, but don't relate to her love of princess play. Ruth and Connie dressed her in pink crepe and gauze gowns, which she refused to change for playgroup, playground, or shopping. We all indulged her fancy, just as we had Dave's cowboy outfits as a boy. She wore her plastic tiara and plastic slippers with rhinestones. Now and again, she waved a flashing toy wand. She built only castles with blocks. Her crayon drawings were all princesses.

More than Eva ever had, she went into deep solitary play. She also hid under tables, and then built private enclosures from blankets or table cloths tied to frame chairs. When she had tantrums she screeched like the Duchess's baby in *Alice in Wonderland*. We went through a phase of playing with jigsaw puzzles together. I admired her intentness and stubborn independence in choosing and fitting the fragments herself. She was only allowed into my workspace in the basement when Ruth or Connie came down to do laundry or bring it up. One of the ironies of my domestic life is that my study is between the cellar stairs and the laundry room, so there is always back and forth and creeping clutter. Both granddaughters are curious about my preoccupation here, similar to Diego's working on his lamps, or working on his MC beats at the computer and turntables. But as their mother had as a child, crawling over barriers to join me in an earlier study: first Eva, then Maya tiptoe down the cellar stairs to invade my space and win me from myself.

Recently, as I sit on the sofa, Maya has taken to climbing from my shoulders to my head, where she no longer feels cute. I tell her no, to stop, I am serious. I ask her if her Dad likes her to climb on his head. Sure, she says.

"Really?"

"My"—she stammers, at a loss—"my grandee from Colombia lets me."

"Grandee Omar?" Diego's father had just visited for a week, his first time in America, and first contact other than on Skype in three years. "I don't think so," I said. "You're a monkey. I'm afraid you'll fall and get hurt."

"Am I five and a half yet?"

"Yes, you turned on May 9, fifteen days ago. You're five and a half and 15 days."

"Finally!"

🌿 🌿 🌿

Eva will remember more. When she was eight, I took her to my office at school, then to nearby Frog Pond on Boston Common to skate. I didn't have enough money to rent two pairs of skates, so I only rented hers. I made sure she was bundled up and mittened. I stood outside the rink's barrier and held her hand, then jogged along as she wobbled forward and the crowd of skaters whizzed past. My face in the audience as she sang and danced in the supporting cast for a childrens' theater production. My straining to listen as she chanted lyrics about justice with Ruth at a hip hop festival and the amplified beat drowned out their words. My coaching her to swim seriously at Walden Pond. Her performing "it's the bare necessities" from Disney's *Jungle Book* for my birthday (I loved puns). I helped her to balance on her first two-wheeler. We watched difficult movies together, such as *To Kill A Mockingbird*. I tried to warn her about materialism when one of her new friends bribed her with expensive gifts, then showed off her own new bike, sneering at Eva's yard-sale one.

Eva's childhood mania had been for dolls, for

dressing them up, for diapering them, for taking them out in a stroller and pushing them in swings. Her play had been little mother play. She looked forward to having a sister, and when Maya arrived, became her parents' helper in caring for her.

"Grandee, why don't you like Poppa Khari?" she asked me once.

"I don't dislike him," I said, thinking he must have told her this. "I don't like his forgetting you. I don't like his breaking promises."

Eva is a dreamer, confident of the world before her. She thrives at school. She takes her parents' hip hop mission in stride. At 12, she is adventurous, going on 21. Given her singing voice, she would be a star. Or she would dance. She would paint. She would write. In sports, she would be a champion, a swimmer, a basketball star, a runner. She would get all A's and go to Harvard. She would be a detective, like Nancy Drew; a lawyer, like Uncle Ray.

She identifies herself as African American. Her sister is Latino. Her friends are mostly children of color. In Colombia, and in Ruth's and Diego's eyes, as in ours, the world is wholesomely diverse. This holds meaning for David, whom we adopted as an infant from Korea, and who says he has always been the target of racism. He celebrates and loves Eva and Maya, and looks at Ruth's married life with admiration. He survives in Manhattan with temporary jobs. He had one serious relationship, but then broke up. We support him and his dream as well as we can. Will I know David's children, I wonder; or if I don't, what will he tell them about me?

We are selves. But we are also vessels. We evolve and devolve. We do each other honor and sometimes offense. The seeds of the future are within each of us, along with inherited wounds and dreams. Times change. Society changes. My mother's feminism and egalitarianism, combined with my father's alcoholic breakdown, encouraged my older sibs and me to reject many of our grandfathers' ideas, especially their dreams of dynasty. We defied their prejudices about class, race, place, morality, and material success. Service and art became our goals. In fact, the strongest influences on me, my children and their children have been my mother, my mother-in-law, and my wife.

To me, both my grandfathers were rich. They were generous. They had drinking problems. They had social ambitions. Starting from farm backgrounds, they had risen in the world and made names for themselves. They were successes. They were Presbyterian. They were heads and patriarchs of families, loyal to their wives. They were disappointed in sons they considered weak.

Both claimed Irish roots (along with some Welsh and Scottish). Both attended business schools. Both married young to relatively non-intellectual women (as depicted by Mom): a "hausfrau" in her father's case; a Sister Carrie, on Dad's side.

DeWitt P. Henry had been supported by his father in founding a candy factory; he also followed his father's example as a local civic leader. Jerome Thralls, in contrast, seemed driven by shame for his father, who had deserted their large family. Unlike DeWitt, Jerome prided himself on being self-made. Both were organizers and innovators. Both were personable, resourceful, tenacious, and able to persuade their peers to collaborate.

Both were products of America's Gilded Age and the Progressive Generation. Both cast long shadows.

Grandpop Henry died when I was seven. As his namesake, I inherited such monogramed items as a humidor, a gold-plated pocket watch, tie clasps, cufflinks and leather brief cases. I also felt important to see my name on the stationery and candy wrappers from the factory. The factory was his legacy, first for my father and then for any of us who sought to take over when my father retired (none of us did, so eventually my father sold out.) I belonged to the third generation of Henrys to be raised in Wayne, PA.

Grandpop Thralls, who owned a Wall Street brokerage and lived in Brooklyn, I visited a few times with Mom. I was seventeen when he died. My mother was his executrix and brought home his papers in four heavy filing cabinets. She narrowed these down to two storage boxes of various items, which she passed to me in case I wanted to write about our family. Clearly, he had prided himself on himself, and meant to be remembered, both by us and by the world.

❧❧ ❧❧ ❧❧

There were multiple, yellowed copies of a full-page interview in the Brooklyn's *Sunday Eagle Magazine* in 1926, where he sounded like Willy Loman's successful brother. His advice was to be a self-starter.

There were posed headshot photographs of him at 25, 35, 39, 56. Him in the *NY Times* feature page teeing off for the Siwanoy Country Club Snowbird Tournament. There was his formal resume as of 1943, where he emphasized that every change in his career was "an advancement." There were letters and notes; speeches in manuscript, speeches reprinted; his text book from

1916, published by the American Bankers' Association (still a text on Amazon), *The Clearing House*; a check for $1., for a year's work at Washington during World War One; a handwritten note on Clearing House stationery, dated 12-7-1903 for "Miss Garlich" (Nana's maiden name), beginning to "My Dear Little Girl" and apologizing for being late for their date; report cards from Chillicothe High School in 9th grade, in 1900, all A's; his 1928 letter of resignation from the Discount Corporation; letters of dispute with the Secretary of the Treasury in 1956 over his right to a government pension, including letters of support from Jesse Jones, whom he addressed as "The Boss"; also Jesse Jones's 1951 book about the RFC, *Fifty Billion Dollars*, where Jones gave tribute to him for recovering an RFC loan to the Prudence Company of New York, a mortgage loan company, dating from the 1930s. Thanks to Grandpop, the RFC realized a $15 million profit. There were letters from Arthur Eisenhower (Dwight's brother), an old friend from Kansas City banking days; from Thomas E. Dewey thanking Grandpop "for the good things you say about my public service"; and best wishes from Missouri's Senator Stuart Symington, Truman's new Administrator of the RFC.

These artifacts and details impressed me. He'd had traits that I recognized in my mother. "Rising in the world" meant making a contribution to society, and in his case, to the systems of banking credit and the economy. He understood big money and how to make it work. Credit, he believed, had to do with character, industry, and trust. At the same time, he warned against buying stocks on margin and giving loans without collateral. His advocacy of the Federal Reserve system had been to prevent bank failures; later his work for the RFC was dedicated to recapitalizing banks and stimulating lending after the start of the Great Depression. He wanted his country to thrive.

But he'd also been an overbearing father. He'd opposed Mom's going to college, even after her principal wrote: "Miss Thralls is a capable, conscientious student of more than ordinary ability....She is just the type of girl that ought to go to our best colleges." Grandpop had insisted: "College isn't for women." Nor was a paying job. She could volunteer, yes, which she did for Travelers' Aid, but paid work for a woman was socially unseemly.

Nonetheless, she was his favorite. He admired her intellect and will. He discussed his business problems with her, had her read his speeches, and even took her to formal business events instead of Nana, who embarrassed him. Finally, he relented and let her go to Cornell, where her older brother had friends, one of whom became my father. Although she quit Cornell in junior year, attended secretarial school, and then art school, Dad and Mom only started dating after Dad had graduated and started as a chemist at Dupont in Newark. He impressed her as stable and down to earth, especially since her previous relationships had been with a murderer (she told us) and then an alcoholic. Grandpop was unimpressed by Dad and had looked down on the Henrys, their candy business, and their social pretensions.

My sister believes that Mom had to get married. This, of course, is contrary to Mom's telling me that she had been a virgin when she married; that that had been the morality of the times. In fact, Mom had shown me a letter from Dad then, saying "no having before the wedding." Their wedding was to have been in October, but suddenly Grandpop had had to make a speech in California on that date, so they cancelled the larger wedding that Mom had planned and moved up the date for a "small family wedding" (her words).

As far as I know, they never asked Grandpop for money. Dad always assumed that Grandpop would leave Mom wealth (Dad's own inheritance from Grandpop Henry had been stock in the factory), but by the time Grandpop Thralls died, any fortune was gone. Instead, Mom inherited the responsibility for Nana Thralls. She and Nana had nothing in common, she felt. She wrote me then: "As a child, I ignored her and became independent early, because she never could answer questions and never had time to listen or pay any attention. She was either sick or busy with my brothers. So early in life I used to tell her I must have been adopted, because she never could be a mother to me. It must have hurt her, but from then on I used teachers and books as my mother. I did not like her. I felt sorry for her inadequacies and sorry for my father because he kept on studying and learning and developing and she didn't make any effort at all to grow with him. I was proud of his achievements, but ashamed of her lack of interest in anything beyond her boys and her naps and shopping. I was always embarrassed about my parents' home. So was my father."

Eventually, they moved Nana Thralls into a nursing home, where she outlived Dad by two years, and Nana Henry by nine, dying in 1978. Except for visits from children and grandchildren, landscapers, tradesmen, and a weekly maid, Mom lived alone until her death in 1985.

❧ ❧ ❧

As I prepare to retire, I have these stories to pass down, although I doubt my children or their children will care. The same is true of my own life's legacy, public and private.

Memories fade, even of those dearest to us. That's how it should be, probably. Mom passed down her boxes of memorabilia, but I wonder if they are worth saving for future generations. Do we need more than a handful of posed snapshots, outlines, caricatures, and legends? Does it matter whether Mom married because she was pregnant or whether she was a virgin? It is time to move on.

I hope to see my grandchildren learn and grow. I hope as adults that they are kind, and lucky, funny and resourceful, and find the world hospitable and wide. I imagine their gifts of body and soul. I imagine them beyond imagining, yet always familiar. I hope they live full lives, involved in lives. I hope that they find their own balance between service, ambition and love. And should they read these words, that they will recognize something of themselves in me, as well as in their parents, Connie, and their many-sided heritage.

Grandee, indeed. Dayenu, dayenu!

A NOTE ON MY POEM
"ANDREW WYETH"

My first close-up experience of an Andrew Wyeth painting was "Wind From the Sea," which hung on loan in my college's art museum when I was a freshman. An open, weathered window frame (probably from inside Christina Olson's house in Maine), with ragged, tattered curtains lifted by a breeze. "Ordinary," commentators point out; yet rich with drama and meticulous caring and invention on the artist's part, all that detail! Curtain fibers, like...well, hair. Or wild sea grass. And haunted by the painter's emotions, and by the invisible forces of nature. A breath of spring.

In decades that followed, I absorbed what I assumed then to be the Wyeth oeuvre. A hundred or so paintings reproduced in *Life* magazine, then collected in books, following on curated exhibitions, etc. Publication of his long-hidden series, *The Helga Pictures,* caused a stir in 1987. Wyeth died in 2009, but it was not until after his wife and executor Betsy's death in 2020 that as many as 10,000 images (paintings, sketches, and notebook studies) became public.

Since then, I've followed a Facebook page dedicated

to Wyeth, and a seemingly inexhaustible feed of unfamiliar Wyeths. I've come to realize how mannered his subjects and compositions could be, so at times he seems to be imitating himself. But also how he kept working at given subjects, version after version, until inspiration kicked in.

He spiritualized a lived domestic and local world, with objects, perspectives, and props of daily use. He loved eternal forces, of light, of wind, of heat and cold, of time itself, and how they met and shaped resistances. In "Monday Morning," what is the drama of an oval wicker wash-basket left out and leaned lengthwise against an outside wall? Remnants of snow remain in its bottom curve. Its season of human use is just returning, announced by morning sunlight striking it slant, and casting its striated and elongated shadow across the ground and up the improbable angles of a triangle-shaped basement bulkhead. Sun meets wicker and casts a shadow seemingly beyond prediction, and which even suggests menace as it ends in a sharp point. Wyeth and Robert Frost were mutual admirers, I've read, sharing a sense of commonplace shocks and recognitions.

Ekphrastic poetry usually pays "inter-media" respect to visual art, from Achilles' shield in Homer to the Grecian Urn in Keats's Ode. My poem, however, seeks to evoke an experience that Wyeth never noticed or imagined, yet which is reinforced, if not inspired by his example.

The phenomenon my poem describes is one I have never noticed before in nature or in art: a reflection, caused by fall sunlight, off a window near running water and cast as a glowing replica, like a fixed and floating carpet, on a constant wave of fast-spilling current: a natural marvel of choreography, the mystery of which is contradiction.

ACKNOWLEDGEMENTS

Perspectives (*Solstice*, July 2010)

First Love (*Agni* #49, 1999)

Sever Hall (*Woven Tale Press*, 2024)

Cambridge Vignettes (*Wilderness House Literary Review*, Vol. 11, No.3, 2016)

My Own Private Cambridge (*Nebraska Review*, 27/1, Winter 1999)

Promises to Keep (*Ploughshares,*, Fall 2001)

On My Racism (*Ploughshares*, Fall, 1990)

An Inappropriate Man (unpublished)

Writing from Experience (unpublished)

Shamrocks and Salad Days (*Solstice*, 2012)

Saga of a Chair (unpublished)

Affair to Remember (*Celebrities in Disgrace Website*, 9/22/17)

A Tribute to "Tornado At The Club," From Evan S. Connell's MRS. BRIDGE (*Wilderness House Literary Review*, Vol. 5, No. 1, April, 2010. Awarded a **Chekov Prize** as best fiction of the year.

Face to Face (unpublished)

Thoughts on Tillie Olsen (unpublished)

Memories of Henry Bromell (*Ploughshares Blog*, 7/19/19)

Remembering James Alan McPherson (*Ploughshares Blog*, 9/16/18)

On Fact and Fiction (*Woven Tale Press*, 10/10/2018)

"What If?" essay, (*Wilderness House Literary Review*, April 2008)

Replaying Doom (*Speculative Non-fiction*, 12/15/20)

Metadoodle (unpublished)

Dayenu (*Unlikely Stories Mark V*, 9/19/21)

A Note on my Poem, "Andrew Wyeth" (forthcoming in Cassandra Atherton's study of ekphrastic poetry, expected from Princeton Univ. Press, 2026).

DeWitt Henry

DeWitt Henry is the founding editor of the internationally prestigious literary journal, *Ploughshares*.

A prolific writer, his award-winning books span diverse genres, from his latest novel TOP COP KILLS (2026) to his prize-winning novel THE MARRIAGE OF ANNA MAYE POTTS (2024/2001), to his essays THREE (2026), PERSPECTIVES: UNCOLLECTED ESSAYS (2026), SWEET MARJORAM: NOTES AND ESSAYS (2018) to his memoirs, ENDINGS & BEGINNINGS: FAMILY ESSAYS (2021), VISIONS OF A WAYNE CHILDHOOD (2012), SWEET DREAMS: A FAMILY HISTORY (2011), SAFE SUICIDE: ESSAYS, NARRATIVES, AND MEDITATIONS (2008) to his poetry, DO I DREAM OR WAKE? (2025), FOUNDLINGS: FOUND POEMS FROM PROSE (2022), TRIM RECKONINGS (2023), RESTLESS FOR WORDS: POEMS (2023), and half a dozen anthologies, and articles too numerous to list.

Henry's awards include the **Peter Taylor Prize for the Novel, NEA Creative Writing Fellow, PEN Friend to Writers, St. Botolph Club Fellowship, CCLM Editorial Fellow, Semi-finalist for PEN Essay Award, Chekov Award for Fiction** from Wilderness House Literary Review, the **Pushcart Prize** (for memoir), the **Boulevard Prize** (for memoir), and the **Pushcart's 3rd Editor's Book Award**, and Runner-up for the **Sinclair Fiction Prize**, and winner of the **Massachusetts Commonwealth Award.**

He obtained his Ph.D. in English at **Harvard University** and then completed M.F.A. requirements at the **University of Iowa.** He is Professor Emeritus at **Emerson College,** where he has shepherded forth several generations of nationally renowned authors.

Also by DeWitt Henry

Fiction

TOP COP KILLS
Pierian Springs Press, 2026

THE MARRIAGE OF ANNA MAYE POTTS
New Edition with Foreword by Margot Livesey
Pierian Springs Press, June 2024
1ˢᵗ Edition, University of Tennessee Press, 2001
(Winner of the **Peter Taylor Prize for the Novel**)

FALLING: SIX STORIES
CreateSpace, 2016

Essays

THREE
Pierian Springs Press, 2026

PERSPECTIVES: UNCOLLECTED ESSAYS
Pierian Springs Press, 2026

SWEET MARJORAM: NOTES AND ESSAYS
Plume Editions / MadHat Press, 2018

Memoir

Endings & Beginnings: Family Essays
MadHat Press, 2021
(Long-listed for the **PEN/Diamonstein-Spielvogel Award**
for the Art of the Essay, 2022)

Visions Of A Wayne Childhood
CreateSpace, 2012

Sweet Dreams: A Family History
Hidden River Press, 2011

Safe Suicide: Essays, Narratives, And Meditations
Red Hen Press, 2008

Poetry

Do I Dream or Wake?
Pierian Springs Press, November 2025

Trim Reckonings: Poems
Pierian Springs Press, November 2023

Foundlings: Found Poems From Prose
New Edition with Notes, Sources & Full Color Artwork
Pierian Springs Press, October 2023

Restless For Words: Poems
Finishing Line Press, February 2023

Foundlings: Found Poems From Prose
Life Before Man/Gazebo Books, May 2022

Anthologies

SORROW'S COMPANY: WRITERS ON LOSS AND GRIEF
Beacon Press, 2001

BREAKING INTO PRINT: EARLY STORIES AND INSIGHTS INTO GETTING PUBLISHED; A PLOUGHSHARES ANTHOLOGY
Beacon Press, 2000

FATHERING DAUGHTERS: REFLECTIONS BY MEN
(with James Alan McPherson)
Beacon Press 1998, pb. 1999

OTHER SIDES OF SILENCE: NEW FICTION FROM PLOUGHSHARES
Faber and Faber, 1993, o.p.

THE PLOUGHSHARES READER: NEW FICTION FOR THE 80s
(Winner Third Annual Editors Book Award)
Pushcart Press, 1984, NAL, 1985